Vintage Crochet

CHAIN MERCER-CROCHET
20 GRAMMES
50
COATS

Vintage Crochet

Clothing, homewares and more
from the National Library of Australia

CELEBRATING
NATIONAL LIBRARY OF AUSTRALIA PUBLISHING
OVER 50 YEARS

Contents

Totally hooked

If you're addicted to crochet, blame the French: crochet—the term is derived from the French word for 'hook'—probably began as an adjunct of lace-making in France sometime in the sixteenth century. In the seventeenth century, a crochet hook was used to pull loops of thread (usually silk) through each other, at first as a way of joining pieces of lace, but soon the craft developed to create lacy fabrics. Meanwhile, in eighteenth-century Scotland, crafters used a 'shepherd's hook' to work with wool yarn and the result was known as 'shepherd's knitting'.

The first published instructions for crocheted items appeared in a Dutch magazine, the aptly name *Penélopé*, in the early nineteenth century: three patterns for purses crocheted in silk using chain stitch, slip stitch and double crochet (*dubbelde hekelsteek*—literally double hedge stitch) to make different designs.

AS TIME GOES BY

Early crocheted pieces used the same coloured silks that were favoured by the lace-makers who developed the craft and the women who used the items. By the Victorian era, white was the preferred colour for the lacy crocheted accessories that were being produced, often in cotton now that fibre was being imported into Europe from the colonies.

In the first half of the twentieth century, crochet was still very much used for lace-making, in homewares and small lacy personal accessories, although some crochet in wool was beginning to be seen in crocheted blankets and rugs. The postwar availability of synthetic fibres such as rayon and acrylic yarns allowed for the development of bright new colours and inexpensive yarns. However, it was the swinging sixties and seventies that really saw crochet blossom into a significant fashion statement. Crochet clothing and accessories capitalised on the new casual vibe in groovy colours and the hypnotic mandala-style art that exemplified that era.

Like other crafts and home-made clothing, crochet went into abeyance in the last two decades of the twentieth century, when it was generally considered an old-fashioned craft not in keeping with the corporate mentality and sophisticated fashions of the time.

There has been serious interest in reviving and rejuvenating the craft in the twenty-first century, with more interesting yarns and materials now available. Covid-19 lockdowns in the early 2020s also drove significant growth in the practice of fibre arts like knitting and crochet, especially among younger generations.

JOIN THE CHAIN GANG

Chain stitch is the most basic crochet stitch and consists of a loop being pulled through the loop on the hook. Slip stitch is simply a chain stitch that is worked through a previous stitch at the same time as the loop on the hook.

Double crochet stitch starts with a loop on the hook, then you put the hook through a stitch in the row below, wrap the yarn over the hook and pull a loop through so you have two loops on the hook, then wrap the yarn over the hook and pull a new loop through both loops on the hook. In the USA, this is known as single crochet, likely because the stitch is completed in a single motion after the loops have been placed on the hook.

The next most complicated stitch is the treble stitch. To make this stitch, start with a loop on the hook, then wrap the yarn over the hook before inserting the hook into a previous stitch and pulling through a loop. You now have three loops on the hook, hence the UK English name 'treble'. Complete the stitch by pulling a new loop through the first two of these loops, so there are now still two loops on the hook, then wrap the yarn over the hook again and pull a loop through the remaining two loops. In the USA, this is called a double crochet, again, likely due to the two pull-through motions needed to complete the stitch once the loops are on the hook.

You can create longer stitches than the treble, sometimes called double and triple treble (or treble and double treble in the USA), by wrapping the yarn twice or three times around the hook before pulling the loop through the fabric.

GETTING MORE COMPLICATED AND LACY

The basic yarn-over-hook, pull-loop-through stitches of crochet can be used to create all sorts of different effects. Networks of chain stitches joined by slip stitches and double crochet create a lacy mesh fabric, as in the bikini cover-up (page 62). This also features picots around the edges. Picots, which originated in lace-making, are little knobbly stitches made by working chain stitches back into the tops of previous stitches.

Cluster stitches are created by working multiple stitches into the same hole or stitch in the row below. They can be made in the shape of fans, as it is in one of our mod collars (page 100), or bobbles, as in the hot-water bottle cover (page 32), or even by pulling up elongated loops and chain-stitching them together at the top, as in the winter coat (page 48).

HOW TO USE THIS BOOK

If you've never crocheted before—or you learned long ago but have forgotten how—the best way to learn is to find a friend or relative who can teach you face to face. If that's not possible, many yarn and craft stores offer lessons for small groups. Another alternative is to use the internet, where experienced crocheters have posted video tutorials showing you how to get started. Just type 'learn to crochet' into the search box and follow the links down the rabbit hole until you find a teacher whose style suits you. These video tutorials can also be a good resource if you're an experienced crocheter trying a new type of stitch pattern.

USING VINTAGE PATTERNS

Vintage crochet patterns like the ones in this book can be challenging. One of the most common problems people encounter is assumed knowledge; in the twentieth century when many of these patterns were published, the pattern writers and editors thought that most of their readers would be fairly experienced, so they often didn't bother to define their terms and explain how to achieve certain effects. For example, the original pattern for the winter coat (page 48) gave the following instructions for making the lining: 'Cut lining at this point and proceed as desired'. In other words, they expected you to know what kind of fabric to use, how much you would need, what shape the pieces needed to be cut to and how to both sew them together and attach them to the inside of the coat. In this book, we've tried to fill in some of the gaps to make the patterns easier to follow for a modern, perhaps not-so-experienced crafter.

TENSION OR GAUGE

For projects crocheted in one piece, it's impossible to emphasise enough the importance of making a test swatch to check your tension or gauge. This is a small sample of fabric created using the main yarn, stitches and hook size of the pattern. You should make it at least 10 cm square, and check it carefully against the desired size of the finished piece. If it's too small, try going up a hook size; if it's too big, try going down a hook size. If you need to go up or down more than one hook size, you may be using the wrong type of yarn, so try thinner or thicker yarn to achieve the tension you need.

After you make up a sample, wash it and block it (see Finishing the garment, page 11) and lay it flat (without stretching it) on an ironing board or folded towel. Use a ruler or tape measure to measure a 10 cm square in the centre of the swatch and mark it with pins. Now you can count the number of stitches between the pins across the row, and compare it with the number of stitches recommended for the pattern. Similarly, you can count the number of rows between the pins at top and bottom. If the number of stitches (and rows) is the same as recommended, or will give you the size desired, you are all set.

HOOK SIZES

Like knitting needles, crochet hooks used to be numbered by their gauge: this is the diameter (thickness), measured as if they were wire. The number indicates how many diameters fit across an inch, so the larger the number, the thinner the hook. (Note that it is the thickness of the part near the hook rather than the thickness of the shaft that is important in crochet, because stitches are not held on the hook as they are in knitting. This is why you can often see hooks with thicker ergonomic handles that allow easier manoeuvring and reduce strain on wrist tendons.) Originally made of bone, ivory or wood, modern crochet hooks may be made of plastic, aluminium or bamboo, among other materials.

These days, hooks are measured and numbered in millimetres, which makes it easier. The fine steel hooks still associated with lace crochet today used to be needles with a bent end, embedded in wooden or bone handles. The table below shows the fine steel hook equivalents in millimetres, old numbers and US sizes.

Millimetres	Old numbering	US sizes
0.60		16
0.75		14
1.0	6½	11
1.25	5½	10
1.5	4½	8
1.75	4	6

In the USA, the numbers for crochet hooks used to go from 0 (thin) to 15 or so (thick), and modern US hooks tend to use a letter system that goes from B (fine, about 2.25 mm) to S (19 mm). The table at right shows the equivalent crochet hook sizes in diameter in millimetres, old gauge numbers and modern US terms.

Millimetres	Old gauge	US sizes
2.0	14	
2.25	13	B/1
2.5	12	
2.75	--	C/2
3.0	11	
3.25	10	D/3
3.5	9	E/4
3.75	--	F/5
4.0	8	G/6
4.5	7	
5.0	6	H/8
5.5	5	I/9
6.0	4	J/10
6.5	3	K/10.5
7.0	2	
7.5	1	
8.0	0	L/11
9.0	00	M/13
10.0	000	N/15

YARN CHOICE

One of the difficulties in using a vintage pattern is finding a modern equivalent of the original yarn. Few of the yarns recommended for the patterns in this book are still available and the ways of describing the thickness (or ply) are no longer the same. For example, the winter coat pattern (page 48) recommends 12-ply yarn: we used 10-ply and found that we achieved the correct tension.

In order to work out what thickness of yarn to use, it's better to look at the recommended hook size and tension (stitch count). Here's where making a test swatch to check your tension is important.

In general, the following hook sizes apply:

Yarn weight	Hook size
Pearl cotton nos. 5, 8, and 12	1.50–2.00 mm or smaller
2-ply (lace)	2.00 mm
3-ply (baby)	2.75–3.00 mm
4-ply (fingering)	3.00–3.50 mm
5-ply (sport)	3.25–4.00 mm
8-ply (double knitting or DK)	3.50–4.50 mm
10-ply (aran, worsted)	5.00–6.00 mm
12-ply (heavyweight)	6.50–7.50 mm
14-ply (bulky)	7.00–9.00 mm
Super chunky or jumbo	10.00 mm and above

Try to select yarn of similar composition to that suggested in the original pattern; that is, if the pattern recommends 100 per cent wool, choose a modern 100 per cent wool yarn. Many people prefer to crochet with cotton or sustainable bamboo yarns, but be aware that even if your test swatch is correct, the different qualities of the yarn mean that the garment may not drape or stretch like the original.

MEASURING UP

Vintage patterns were not designed in the range of sizes that we expect in modern patterns, and in general, people today are taller and wider. Compare your body measurements carefully with those given in the pattern, and don't forget to make a test swatch to check that the finished garment will be the size you want.

If you want to change the size of the garment from that given in the pattern, on the next page there are some simple tips on how to do it.

- To go up one size (about 5 cm larger), use a hook one size larger than recommended. Make sure you make a test swatch with the larger hook and count the stitches, then you can work out the finished dimensions of the garment to check that the new size will be correct. To do this, count the number of stitches over 10 cm in your larger test swatch. Divide the desired measurement of the garment by 10. Multiply by the number of stitches in the swatch to check that the new number is close to the number of stitches in the pattern. Don't forget to check the row count; some patterns tell you to work a certain number of rows rather than a length in centimetres.
- To go down one size (about 5 cm smaller), use a hook one size smaller than recommended and check the measurements against your test swatch as above.
- If you want to increase by two sizes (10 cm) or more, it's better to add stitches and rows where you need them. This is easier if it's a plain crochet fabric or the pattern has a small repeat, but if it's a lacy or complicated pattern, you might not want to attempt adding stitches unless you are confident. Make sure that you increase in multiples of the pattern repeat if there is one. To work out how many stitches to add, make a test swatch to check the stitch count. If you want to add 20 cm to the chest measurement of the garment, you'll need to add 10 cm each to the front and back, so add the number of stitches you counted in your test swatch. Don't forget to consider the additional stitches when it comes time to cast off for armholes or necklines. It may be helpful to draw out the tricky parts of the pattern (such as armholes) on graph paper so you can work out how to decrease with the additional stitches. Remember that you will also need to increase the width and length of sleeves.
- If you want to decrease by two sizes (10 cm) or more, apply the same principles as for increasing, subtracting stitches and rows as necessary.
- See the chapter on granny squares (page 13) to make garments smaller or larger by adding squares or using thinner or thicker yarn.

When converting from imperial (inches) measurement in the original patterns to metric (centimetres) we used the following approximate conversions:

Inches	**Centimetres**
1	2.5
2	5
3	7.5
4	10
5	13
6	15
7	18
8	20
9	23
10	25.5
12	30.5
14	36
16	40.5
18	46
20	51
25	63.5
30	76
32	81
34	86
36	92
38	96.5
40	102

FINISHING THE GARMENT

When all of the pieces of the garment are made, you'll need to sew them together. Use the same yarn, and thread it into a wool needle with a large eye and a blunt point. Some people like to use ladder or mattress stitch, which is worked with the pieces laid flat, right side up. Others prefer a backstitch seam, sewn with the right sides of the fabric together. Still others like to use crochet to join two pieces of fabric with a slip stitch at strategic points (see the hot-water bottle cover on page 32) or using double crochet (see the afghan on page 24). If you do this, the seam can be a feature of the garment on the outside or you can work it on the inside to make it invisible.

After the garment is assembled, the final step is to block it. To do this, lay a thick towel or cloth on a flat surface. Dampen the garment by spraying it with cool water or handwashing it. Spread it out on the towel, gently pulling it into shape. Leave it to dry flat in the shade. Some of the patterns in this book recommend using an iron on the wool setting and a cloth to press the garment from the wrong side.

GARMENT CARE

Modern yarns will often be machine-washable. Wool and other natural fibres, such as silk, mohair and alpaca, that are not labelled machine-washable can be handwashed in lukewarm or cool water, using a gentle soap or detergent. There are specialty woolwash soaps and detergents available, some of which don't even need to be rinsed out of the garment as they provide a protective layer to the yarn.

Do not wring out a crocheted garment or peg it on a clothesline to dry. Instead, press as much water as you can out of the fabric using your hands and then lay it on a thick towel. Roll it up in the towel and squeeze; the towel will absorb a lot of the water. Lastly, lay it flat on a dry towel or blocking mat and gently pull it into shape without stretching it. Leave it to dry in the shade.

ABBREVIATIONS

We have used the following abbreviations.

beg beginning
ch chain
cont continue
dc double crochet (US single crochet)
dec decrease (subtract a stitch): this is usually achieved by working two stitches together
dtr double treble (US treble), sometimes also called long treble (ltr)
htr half treble: work as for treble but pull loop through all three loops on hook
inc increase (add a stitch): the method often used is to work two stitches into the same stitch below
k knit
p purl
patt pattern
prev previous
rep repeat
sl-st slip stitch
sp space (usually the space created by crocheting a chain stitch instead of a dc or tr)
tog together
tr treble (US double crochet)
yoh yarn over hook

NOTE ON CONTENT

Women's crafts and domestic labour are intrinsically linked with feminism. Artists and activists have long used crochet to protest the mistreatment of women and draw attention to women's issues and other matters. Please be advised that some of the textboxes contain mature themes and imagery.

Granny squares

With a nod to those matriarchs who may have taught us all we know about crochet, these days crocheted squares or 'motifs' are known to most as 'granny squares'. These motifs are the basic building blocks for many crochet projects.

Most people begin their crocheting practice with simple squares that use various forms and groupings of the basic stitches to make colourful textures and patterns. These squares can be sewn (or crocheted) together to create everything from blankets (see page 24) to dresses (see pages 20 and 28).

The technique for making a square begins with a ring of chain stitches, or sometimes a magic ring—if you can't find someone to teach you how to make a magic ring, the internet is your friend—into which the first round or row of stitches is worked. By working more rounds of stitches and adding extra stitches at the corners, you increase the complexity of the square (or, indeed, the triangle, hexagon or circle, depending on the number of corners you make). Using different decorative stitches or colours in each successive round also adds interest.

Multiple squares can be joined together to make larger and more complex shapes, as in the projects on the following pages.

Once you get the hang of making squares and joining them into different configurations, the sky's the limit. Go get grannying!

Experienced

Motif cardigan

Small motifs in multiple bright colours contrast with black borders to make a stunning, easy-to-wear cardigan.

The Australian Woman's Mirror, 9 June 1954.

Materials: 4-ply wool yarn, 50 g balls: 4 x black, 1 x each of 8 other colours; 2.75 mm crochet hook; 5 buttons.
Measurements: To fit 86 cm bust; length from shoulder 46 cm. Each motif measures 5 cm across. 286 motifs will be needed.
Special stitches: Cluster: 3 tr, leaving last loop of each on hook, then draw a loop through all 3 loops together.

MOTIFS

Using 1st colour, make 6 ch, join into ring with sl-st.
1st round: * 3 ch as 1st tr, 2 tr (to make 1st cluster), 2 ch. Rep from * 5 times. Join with sl-st to top of 1st cluster.
2nd round: Change colour. 5 ch, 1 tr on top of 1st cluster, * (1 tr, 2 ch, 1 tr) into 2 ch sp, (1 tr, 2 ch, 1 tr) into top of next cluster. Rep from * all round, finishing (1 tr, 2 ch, 1 tr) into 2 ch sp, join with sl-st to 3rd of 5 ch at beginning of round. Change to black.
3rd round: Work 5 ch, 1 tr in next sp, * (1 tr, 2 ch, 1 tr into next 2 ch sp) twice, 4 ch, (1 tr, 2 ch, 1 tr) into next sp. Rep from *, finishing round with 4 ch, sl-st to 3rd of 5 ch, omitting last (1 tr, ch, 1 tr). Fasten off.

TO JOIN MOTIFS

When working the next motif, on the last round join to prev motif as follows:
3rd round: 5 ch, 1 tr in next sp, 1 ch, sl-st to corresponding ch of prev motif, 1 ch, 1 tr into same 2 ch sp on 2nd motif, (1 tr, 2 ch, 1 tr) into next sp, 2 ch, sl-st to corresponding corner of prev motif, 2 ch.
Connect all motifs in this manner, following the chart on page 17 for position of motifs.

Although this pattern is in one size, you can easily redraw the diagram on page 17 to add extra motif squares to increase the size. In this case, it will be easiest to add extra rows down the centre back and at the front edges. If you're making it larger, you might also want to add rows at the bottom too.

The original 3-ply wool was judged to be equivalent to a modern 4-ply.

Registered in Australia for transmission by post as a newspaper.
Vol. 30—No. 29
Wednesday, June 9, 1954
6D

THE AUSTRALIAN WOMAN'S MIRROR

Gay Crochet Cardigan

(PAGE 12)

THE EDGING

When all the motifs are joined together, work as follows: Using black wool, hold cardigan upside down with the right side of work towards you, and begin at right-hand corner.

1st round: Work 1 dc into each V between sts and 1 dc into each corner sp of motifs all along the lower edge of garment, drawing it up to measure 61–63.5 cm, then work 1 dc into each V and 1 dc between Vs, with 1 dc into each corner sp of motifs on all remaining edges until the starting point is reached.

2nd round: Change colour. 1 dc into 1st dc (3 ch, miss 1 dc, 1 dc into next dc) all round. Sl-st to 1st dc of round and into 1st 3 ch sp.

3rd round: * 3 ch, 1 dc into next sp. Rep from * all round, sl-st to 1st of 3 ch.

4th round: 3 dc into 1st sp, * 1 ch, 3 dc into next sp. Rep from * all round, 1 ch, sl-st to 1st dc.

5th round: Change to black wool. 3 dc into 1 ch sp, * 1 ch, 3 dc into next sp. Rep from * all round, 1 ch, sl-st to 1st dc.

6th round: Change to 2nd edge colour. As 5th round.

7th round: (3 ch, 1 dc into next 1 ch sp) all round, join with sl-st.

8th round: (1 dc into 3 ch sp, 3 ch) all round, join with sl-st.

Break off wool and rejoin to front of next edge, and work (6 ch, 1 dc) into each loop to end of other side of neck edge, turn on to the front edge of garment and work (2 dc into 3 ch sp, 1 dc on dc) all round.

When neck edge is reached, work (3 ch, 1 dc) into each loop all along neck edge, turn on the front edge again and work an edging all round of 3 dc on 3 dc, * 1 picot worked thus: 5 ch, sl-st into 4th ch, then 3 dc on 3 dc. Rep from * all round to neck edge, then to finish neck, work (1 dc, 1 picot, 1 dc) into each sp. Fasten off.

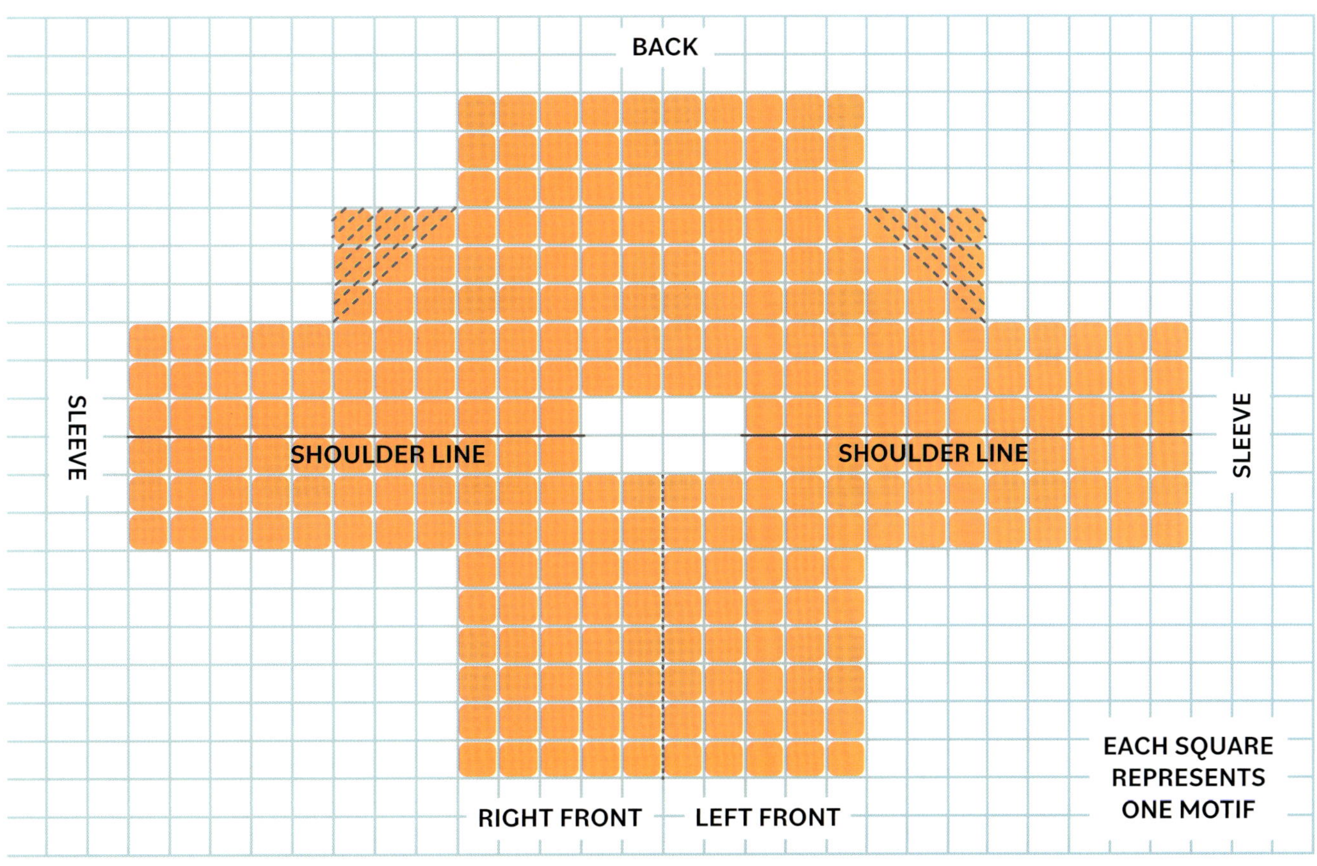

THE CUFFS

Using black yarn, work 1 dc into each V, 1 dc between Vs and 1 dc into each corner sp.
Change to edge colour and work as for body border until 5th round completed.
Change to other edge colour and work as for body border until 8th round completed.
9th round: (6 ch, 1 dc) into each loop, join with sl-st.
10th round: As 9th round.
11th round: (3 ch, 1 dc into next sp) all round, join with sl-st.
Now work as rounds 3–8 of main border and then finish with the picot edge as before.

TO FINISH

If you like, make a chain cord with black wool and run through holes at neck. Make two tassels and sew to ends of cord.
Sew on five buttons down left front and use holes of right front edge as buttonholes. Give garment a press with a hot iron over a damp cloth.

Evolution of the granny square

PATTERN FOR CRAZY AFGHAN.

One of the most versatile and iconic crochet motifs, granny squares allow the crocheter to play with textures, sizes, colours and colour schemes, all while anchored to a simple symmetry. They have long been a staple of needlework, as a way to make use of scraps when wool was scarce, but also a very deliberate and clever way to use crochet in 'crazy work', a trend of using irregular shapes, colours and textures in patchwork quilting that was popular in the late nineteenth century (and again in the late twentieth century).

Some sources suggest that the very first motif was crocheted by a Mrs Phelps from Illinois in 1885. Her pattern for a 'bright and varied' crazy afghan, edged in black, appeared in *The Prairie Farmer*. Only ten years later, in the 'Ladies' Column' of Brisbane's *Telegraph*, the correspondent writes:

> *I want to tell you of my ways of using up scraps of worsted, zephyr, Germantown, etc. From the time I was seven years old crocheting has been my occupation while learning a recitation or lesson, in fact, in committing anything to memory. Consequently, in over ten years' saving of odds and ends, I had on hand a large amount of many different colors …*

Having made an underskirt, she continues:

> *As this did not use up all my wool I crocheted the rest into four-inch squares, which, when joined, made a very pretty afghan, though a trifle 'crazy' looking on account of the numerous colors.*

The hunt for the first Australian granny-square pattern continues (calling all Voluntroves!).

Granny squares have never really gone out of style as a foundation for homewares, particularly bedspreads and blankets, but it wasn't until the 1970s that they were embraced by young people, keen to create handmade clothing and accessories in unique styles. Patterns in women's magazines of this era show classic granny-square designs for tops and cropped vests, and looser examples of self-expression could be seen on the streets in ponchos, flared pants and more. Thrift was in again after the consumerism of previous decades, and 'reduce, reuse, recycle' was gaining ground; granny squares ticked all the boxes.

In 2016, model Gigi Hadid was snapped leaving a Parisian hotel in a Rosetta Getty granny-square cardigan and matching scarf, paired with leather pants and sky-high heels. Granny squares have appeared on runways in Ryota Murakami sweaters and Dolce and Gabbana two-piece suits, and in retail fashion in Romance Was Born dresses and tops and Stella McCartney jumpers.

In her Pepperland Plus Collection, designer Katie Jones incorporated large granny squares into her garments, mixing and (mis)matching the squares' colours, shapes and sizes in high-waisted, flared pants and loose cardigans. Celia B's designs also make a feature of granny squares in everything from swimwear to skirts and jackets, embracing the multicolour of the traditional square but in a clever, cohesive and super-modern palette.

This pattern is in two sizes, but may be made smaller or larger by using a different hook size. You could also add rows of double crochet or treble stitches between the strips of squares. Make one of the motifs, then block it and calculate the finished dimensions carefully.

If extra length is required make seven more motifs in the main colour and one each of centre A, B and C, then join horizontally as before. This will give an extra 9.5 cm in length.

Intermediate

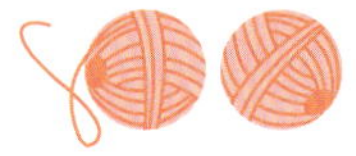

Motif dress

A simple dress with multicoloured motif squares, the shape touches where it pleases in a relaxed shift shape.

The Australian Women's Weekly, 16 November 1966.

Materials: 8-ply (DK) 100% cotton yarn, 50 g balls: 13 x main colour (MC), 1 x each of 3 contrast colours (CC1, CC2 and CC3); 4.00–4.5 mm crochet hook.
Measurements: To fit 86 cm bust; length 94 cm. Each motif measures 9.5 cm square. 86 motifs will be needed.

MOTIFS

Make 6 ch, join into circle with sl-st.
1st round: 3 ch, 15 tr in circle, join with sl-st to 3rd ch.
2nd round: 4 ch, (1 tr in top of tr, 1 ch) 15 times, join with sl-st to 3rd ch.
3rd round: 3 ch, 1 tr in next sp, 2 tr in every sp, join with sl-st to 3rd ch.
4th round: (3 ch, 1 dc in sp between each 2 tr of prev round) rep to end, 3 ch, join with sl-st.
5th round: 3 ch, 1 tr, 1 ch, skip 1 st, 2 tr in ch loop, * (1 ch, 2 tr in next ch loop) 3 times, 1 ch, 4 tr, 1 ch, 4 tr in next ch loop, rep from * 3 times, (1 ch, 2 tr in next ch loop) 3 times, 1 ch join with sl-st to 4th ch and fasten off. (76 st.)
Make 62 motifs in MC only, 6 of which are for the shoulder straps.
Make 8 motifs with circle and 1st round in CC3, 2nd round in MC, 3rd round in CC2, 4th round in CC1, 5th round in MC.
Make 8 motifs with circle and 1st round in CC2, 2nd round in CC1, 3rd round in CC3, 4th round in CC1, 5th round in MC.
Make 8 motifs with circle and 1st round in MC, 2nd round in CC3, 3rd round in CC1, 4th round in CC2, 5th round in MC.

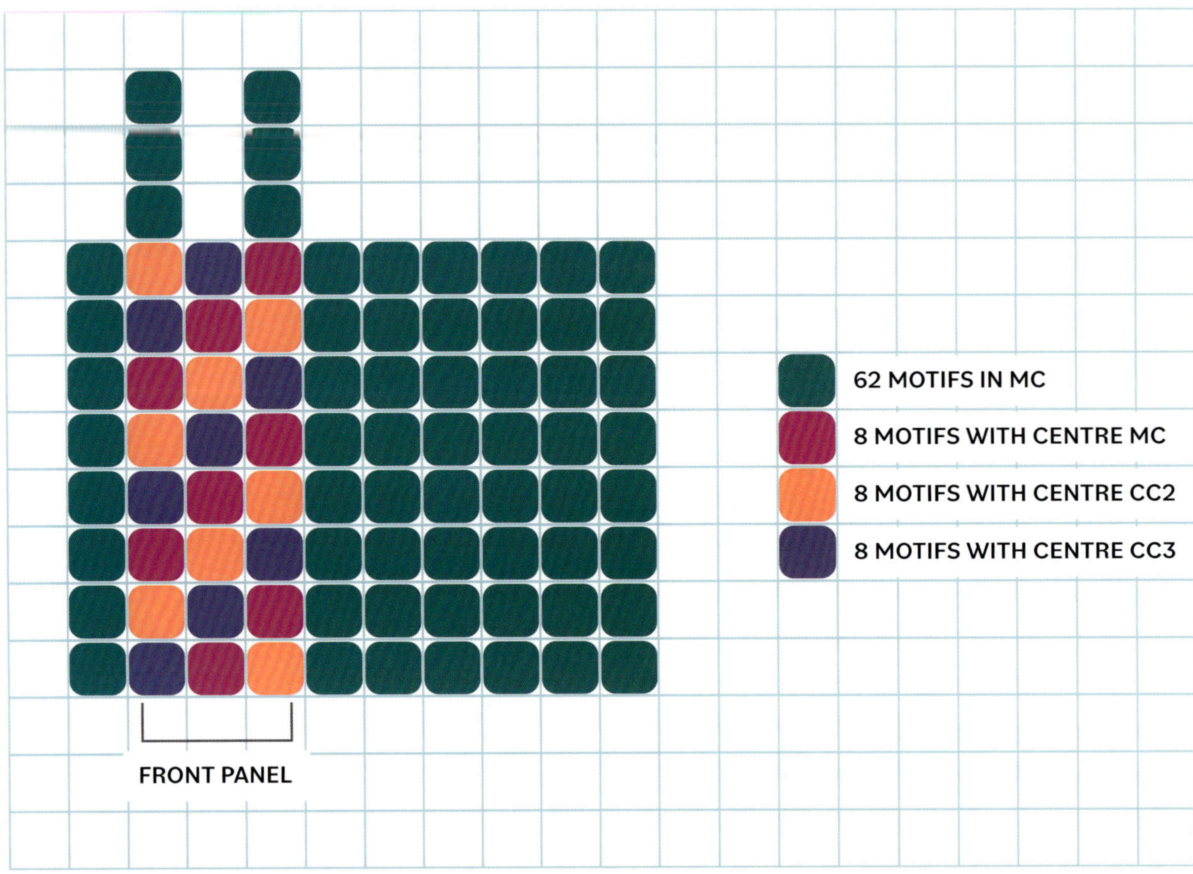

TO MAKE UP

Ensure all squares have been wet blocked to 9.5 cm. Lightly press each motif on wrong side. Proceed to join motifs horizontally (from bottom row) across top edges of row 1 as follows:

* Place 2 motifs in MC only side by side and working along top edges start in top right corner of the 1st motif. Using MC, join in yarn and work (1 dc into 1st corner sp of 1st motif, 4 ch, 1 dc into sp between 2nd and 3rd tr corner of motif, 4 ch, 1 dc into chain sp 4 times, 4 ch, 1 dc into sp between 2nd and 3rd tr corner of motif, 4 ch, 1 dc into corner sp. Rep from * until 6 motifs have been joined. Cont (4 ch, 1 dc) pattern across 1st motif with centre CC2, 1 motif with centre MC, then 1 motif with centre CC1, then 1 motif in MC (10 squares in total). Turn your work and cont across the motifs in reverse, with 2 ch, 1 dc in top of 4 ch, 2 ch, 1 dc into sp between 2nd and 3rd tr corner of motif, (2 ch, 1 dc in top of 4 ch, 2 ch, 1 dc into chain sp) 4 times, 2 ch, 1 dc in top of 4 ch, 2 ch, 1 dc into sp between 2nd and 3rd tr corner of motif, 2 ch, 1 dc in top of 4 ch, 2 ch, 1 dc into corner sp, 2 ch, 1 dc in top of 4 ch, 2 ch, 1 dc into corner sp of motif with centre CC2 and rep until motifs have been joined. End row.

Cont, following the diagram, adding rows horizontally until all 8 rows have been joined. Then work the pattern vertically until all squares have been joined and dress is a tube shape.

TO FINISH

Top edge border: With right side facing, join MC at a corner sp and work 2 ch, 1 dc into every sp to last sp, 2 ch, join with sl-st.

Lower edge border: Work 1 row as for top edge.

Next row: (2 dc, 4 ch sl-st into 1st ch for picot, 2 dc into ch loop) rep to end, join with sl-st and fasten off.

Shoulder straps: At top of the outer motifs of the front panel, join one strap motif to top border, then join a 2nd motif to opposite side of 1st motif, join 3rd motif to opposite side of 2nd motif. Join opposite side of 3rd motif to top border at the back of the dress. Join another shoulder strap in the same way.
Armholes and neck borders: Work as border for lower edge.
Lightly press work on wrong side.

Beginner

Afghan

For sheer comfort, these convenient coverlets have no equal. They are so easy to make. This one is made up of a series of crocheted motifs.

The Australian Women's Weekly, 13 March 1957.

Materials: 4-ply 100% merino wool machine-washable yarn, 50 g balls: 1 x each of 8 varied colours, 2 x each of colours for background and border; 2.50 mm crochet hook.
Measurements: Each motif measures 11 cm square. The completed rug with 90 motifs measures 112 x 124 cm.
Tip: Crochet over the yarn tail as you work the 1st round of each motif. This will allow you to pull the tail and tighten up the ring before cutting the tail off.

MOTIFS

Make 5 ch, join into ring with a sl-st.
1st round: 3 ch, (2 tr, 1 ch, 3 tr) into the ring, (1 ch, 3 tr) into the ring 3 times, 1 ch, join with a sl-st into the 3rd ch at beg of round. (This makes 4 blocks of 3 tr with 1 ch between each.) Sl-st over 2 tr to reach the 1st 1 ch sp.
2nd round: 3 ch, 2 tr, 1 ch, 3 tr into 1st sp, (3 tr, 1 ch, 3 tr) into next 3 sps, join with a sl-st into the 3rd ch at beg of round.
3rd round: Change yarn colour. 3 ch, 2 tr into next sp, (3 tr, 1 ch, 3 tr) into next sp. Cont working 3 tr into each sp with (3 tr, 1 ch, 3 tr) into each corner sp to end of round, 1 ch, join with a sl-st into the 3rd ch at beg of round. Cont in this way, changing colour every 2 rounds until 6 rounds have been worked. Work 1 round of background colour and finish with 1 round of border colour.

TO MAKE UP

When the desired number of motifs for required rug size have been worked, join with a flat seam or crochet together using border colour. Press lightly.

TO FINISH

Edge with 1 round of background colour, 2 rounds of a 2nd colour, 1 round each of a 3rd and 4th colour, and 3 rounds of the border colour, or as desired.

The original pattern gave no yarn weight or quantity and suggested a 2.00 mm crochet hook. Our afghan was made in 4-ply wool yarn using a 2.50 mm hook, but you could also make it in 8-ply yarn using a 4.00 mm hook to make larger motifs. The number of motifs you make will determine the finished size.

Crochet craftivism

The Föhr Reef, a setellite of the Crochet Coral Reef, on display at the Museum of the University of Tübingen in an exhibition called Wie Schönes Wissen schafft (how beauty creates knowledge).

According to American academic Rachel Maines, women have long been using needlework to transmit coded messages to each other, expressing frank sentiments 'protected by the cultural camouflage of needlework's respectability'. Men, she writes, don't know the meaning of symbols and design elements worked into these craft objects and so the messages remain secret among women, and reveal much about women's lives.

Crochet work by feminist artists in the 1970s wanted men to get the memo, and any symbology was accompanied by direct political messaging.

One of the founders of feminist art collective the Women's Domestic Needlework Group was Frances (Budden) Phoenix, who produced crochet doilies with political messages. A 1970s doily asks 'Who killed Juanita?', a reference to missing urban conservation activist Juanita Nielsen. Although the case remains unsolved, Phoenix defiantly answers the question: 'DEVELOPERS'. The piece was designed and worked in political support of Victoria Street Resident Action, at a time when the group was protesting the planned destruction of terrace housing by a developer. Other doilies produced in the 1970s deal with different women's right issues from abortion laws (see page 70) to the plight of women in incarceration. She also reappropriated found doilies, giving a second life to handed-down objects and turning the idea of crochet as domestic or stuffy on its head. Nothing could be further from the original use of a doily than Phoenix's 1975 artwork *Queen of Spades*, but both are equally feminine!

The Crochet Coral Reef project by Australian sisters Christine and Margaret Wertheim is an artistic response to climate change that travels to museums and galleries around the world. The medium is part of the message: crochet takes time and time is running out. The crocheted reefs are both 'militantly un-tech' and yet were made using 'some of humanity's oldest, most critical *technes*' in the form of the crochet hook:

> *These artworks reflect the history of handicrafts traditionally done as a means of necessity but now being embraced by the art world as a way of claiming—or rather reclaiming—the aesthetic power of 'fancywork'. For of course, handicrafts have always been aesthetic tools rich in symbolism and expressive possibility, and 'ladies' doing their embroideries have long been artists, even if they are rarely acknowledged as such.*

Alongside the original collection, satellite reefs, constructed by more than 20,000 volunteer crocheters, have sprung up everywhere, from the UAE to Melbourne.

Today, crochet is still used to pack a punch. In 2023, Blacktown craftivists said no to domestic violence for the fifth year in a row by yarnbombing public spaces with knitted and crocheted squares, sewn together. The goal was vibrant visibility.

The pattern is only in one size, but can be sized up (or down) by adding or omitting a row of motifs from the centre front and back. More subtle size changes can be obtained by going up or down a hook size: work a motif, block it and calculate the measurements carefully.

Intermediate

Antimacassar dress

A supple little shape caught at the waist with a ribbon, the motifs in this dress are reminiscent of the protective doilies that were draped over the back of chairs to prevent staining with macassar hair oil.

The Australian Women's Weekly, 16 March 1966.

Materials: 5-ply (sport) soft cotton, 23 x 50 g balls; 3.25 mm crochet hook; 1.5 m of satin ribbon, 2 cm wide.
Measurements: To fit 86 cm bust; length 92 cm. Each motif measures 7.5 cm square.

MOTIF

Make 6 ch and join into ring with sl-st.
1st round: 3 ch (turning ch counts as 1st dtr throughout), 11 dtr into ring, join with sl-st.
2nd round: Sl-st to next sp, 3 ch, dtr, 1 ch, 2 dtr into same sp, *3 ch, skip 3 sts, 2 dtr, 1 ch, 2 dtr. Rep from * 2 more times, 3 ch, join with sl-st to 1st st (four corners).
3rd round: Sl-st to next sp, 3 ch, 2 dtr, 1 ch, 3 dtr into same sp, * 4 dtr into 3 ch sp, 3 dtr, 1 ch, 3 dtr into corner. Rep from * 2 more times, 4 dtr into 3 ch sp, join with sl-st to 1st st.
4th round: Sl-st to between 1st 2 dtrs of prev round, 3 ch, 1 dtr, 1 ch, 1 dtr into corner sp, *working into sps between sts of prev round, 1 dtr in each of next 2 sps, 2 dtr into next sp, 1 dtr in each of next 3 sps, 2 dtr into next sp, 1 dtr in each of next 2 sps, 1 dtr, 1 ch, 1 dtr in corner sp. Rep from * 2 more times until round is finished, join with sl-st and fasten off.
Make 184 motifs.

TO MAKE UP

Wet block and pin out motifs to 7.5 cm square. Neatly sew motifs together with flat seams, working to below diagram of single side where each square represents 1 motif.

Sew upper arm, underarm and side seams, leaving space for neck opening. Press work on wrong side.

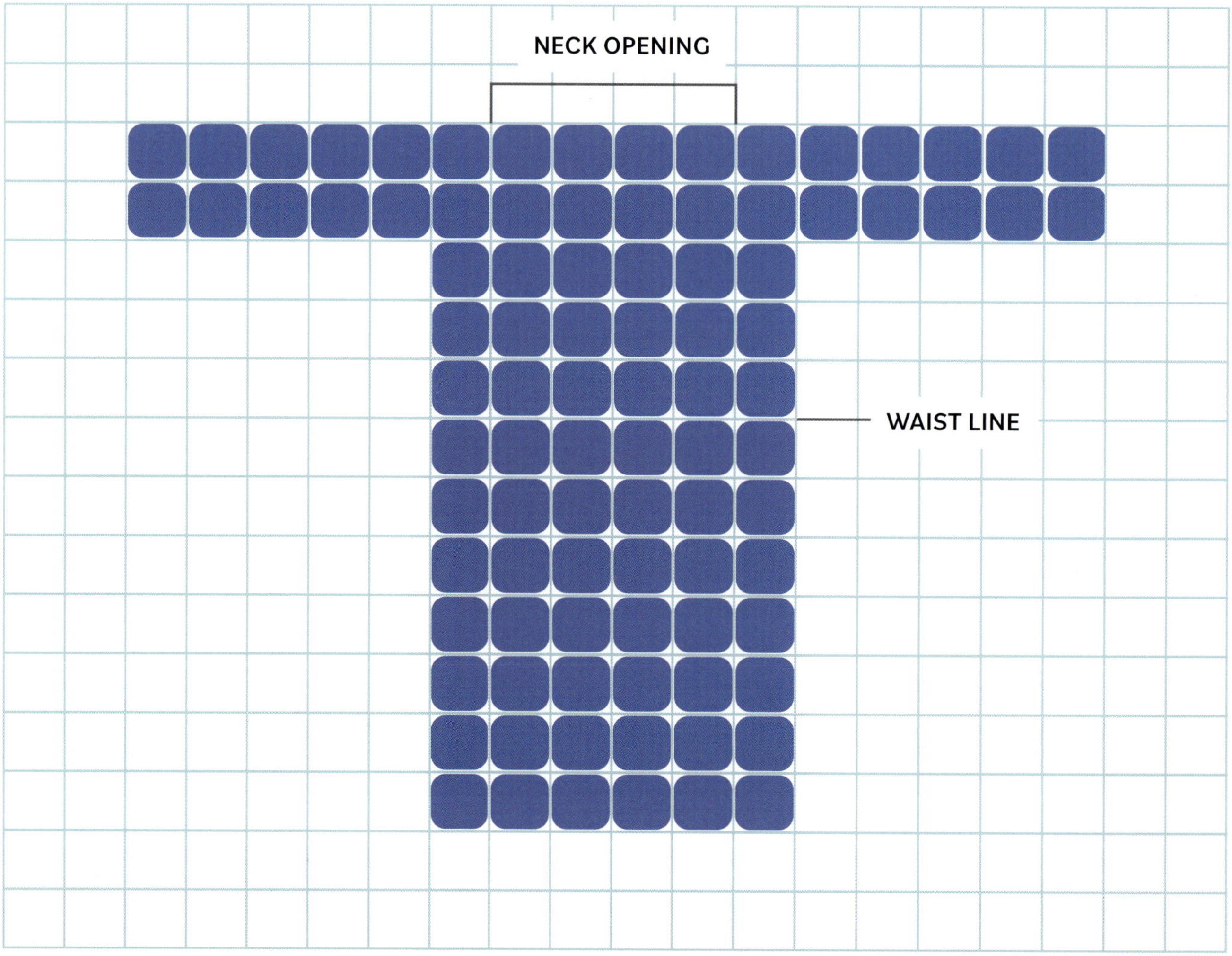

NECK OPENING

WAIST LINE

A N T IMACASSAR DRESS (above left), a supple little shape caught at the waist with a tie of bright ribbon, is made from 184 little crocheted squares. Directions on page 18.

Beginner

Hot-water bottle cover

Use these wool crochet squares for rugs, shawls or hot-water bottle covers!

The Australian Woman's Mirror, 16 June 1936.

Materials: 4-ply sock yarn, 20 g balls: 2 x dark colour and 2 x light colour; 3.25 mm crochet hook.
Measurements: Each motif measures 9 cm square. 15 motifs will be needed.
Special stitches: Long treble (ltr): wrap yarn twice over hook before putting it through the stitch below; tuft: 4 tr into same place, withdraw hook from loop, insert into 1st tr, bring loop through, then work 1 ch tightly.

MOTIF

1st round: 12 ch, join into a ring with sl-st. 3 ch, 23 tr into the ring (24 sts).
2nd round: Change colour. Work 1 tuft into every 3rd tr, with 5 ch between.
3rd round: Change colour. Work 6 tr over every 5 ch and 1 ch over every tuft.
4th round: Change colour. * Miss 2 tr of 6 tr group, 1 tr into each of next 4 tr, 1 tr over 1 ch, 1 tr into each of 1st 4 tr of next group, 6 ch, 1 ltr into 1 ch, 6 ch. Rep from * 3 times, join with sl-st into 1st tr and end off.
Make 15 motifs.

TO MAKE UP

To join motifs as you go, join with sl-st at corner ltr and 1st, 5th and 9th tr along the side, and at next corner ltr, to corresponding stitches of prev square.
To make a hot-water bottle cover, work a piece consisting of 5 rows of 3 motifs. Join the ends with a flat seam and fold so the seam is at centre back, and the centre front is a full motif.
Lower edge: Work 1 dc into each tr, 3 dc into corner chain sps, 1 dc into each sp in the 'star' corners. Fold flat and join front and back along lower edge with a row of dc. If your hot-water bottle has a hanging tab, leave a gap of about 4 cm in the centre.
Top edge, 1st row: 1 tr into every tr and 3 tr into every 5 ch loop.
2nd row: 3 tr into every 3rd tr.
3rd row: * 3 tr into sp between 3 tr group in prev row, work 3 ch, 1 dc back into 2nd tr (to make a picot). Rep from * to end. Fasten off.
For the tie, use doubled yarn to crochet a chain about 75 cm long. Fasten off. Thread through the sps in the 3rd row and knot the ends.

These versatile motifs use two colours in alternating rows, but you could also make them in one, three or four colours. Using a different weight of yarn and hook size, you can make them smaller or larger too. For small articles, join the squares together as you go, but for large pieces you may work squares separately and sew together last.

Crochet: joining the loops

As first, second and third generations of settlers established themselves in the Australian colonies, the women turned their attentions from survival to leisure. Domestic crafts provided a remedy for boredom; an income source; a way to decorate homes; and a means to create functional household objects.

Crocheted and beaded jug covers were first made to solve a problem of bush life: how to keep flies out of milk. They quickly evolved into little artistic projects, with the crocheter selecting materials to weigh her doily down. As Jennifer Isaacs writes in *The Gentle Arts*:

> *There were everyday beaded covers or ones for entertaining, ornately crocheted with iridescent beads and shells. In a busy country home where evening hours were limited, it was not possible to crochet elaborate covers for milk jugs but old mozzie netting with a simple crocheted edging did the trick.*

Designs for crocheted embellishments were often inspired by the crocheter's immediate surrounds. Just as women painters tended to paint domestic and garden scenes and still-life tableaus, crocheters found inspiration locally, with Australian flora appearing in crochet designs around the same time it was introduced into gardens in the mid-nineteenth century.

The price and availability of cotton in the late nineteenth century meant crochet, particularly lace crochet, was a popular pastime. The Victorian Intercolonial Exhibition of 1875 attracted 240,000 visitors to the State Library of Victoria to see a display of colonial Australia's manufactured goods, produce, arts and achievements. Melbourne's *Argus* of 2 September 1875 reported that alongside an exhibit by the Inspector-General of Penal Establishments of the handiwork of prisoners, including warders' uniforms and even straitjackets, Miss Maria Gay of Spencer Street and Miss Ellen Power of Romsey exhibited 'crochet counterpanes of elegant workmanship', Miss Jane Ann Murray of East Collingwood exhibited 'some wondrously intricate crochet work' and Miss Richmond Henty of Portland exhibited 'the finest point lace crochet sleeves and tatting d'oyley marked by a finish and delicacy of design which are extremely attractive'. The rapidly expanding wool industry had a big influence on the sorts of things produced in crochet. When it kicked into gear, woollen blankets and rugs became popular.

Madame Weigel was one of the first commercial publishers of pattern books in colonial Australia and her business would continue into the late 1960s. By the 1930s, her crochet pattern books were being mass produced and sold cheaply, and included patterns for tea cosies, afghans, egg cosies, cushions, rugs, pram covers and more. Patterns by manufacturers such as the Semco Art Needlework Company, which also produced embroidery fabrics, threads and instruction books, were also readily available, contributing to a crochet boom period in the 1940s. Pattern books and patterns published in women's magazines dictated trends and led innovations in crocheting at a time when major designers were uninterested in the craft.

Tatting—a similar craft to crochet—also made a comeback in the 1930s. Making durable, delicate knotted lace with a shuttle was popular in the last quarter of the nineteenth century, as a way to make edgings, collars and cuffs, doilies, decorative mats and tablecloths. Tatting designer Norma Benporath began to publish patterns in Australian newspapers in the late 1920s before becoming sought after by women's magazines and putting her name to a series of tatting lesson and pattern books published by *The Australian Home Beautiful* in the 1930s.

The popularity of crochet waned with the availability of affordable ready-made clothes and laces after the Second World War, until a second boom period in the 1970s brought crochet back into vogue. Although it has gone in and out of fashion for more than a hundred years, in many homes in Australia today examples of crochet are among those objects handed down from generation to generation. Handmade lace is reused on hems or in hand-me-down baby clothes or moved from the collar of one shirt to another. Single finished granny squares found in an inherited bag of needlework are added to and sewn together to make blankets that carry meaning and history. The project you're crocheting from this book today may be repurposed in some yet unimaginable way a hundred years from now!

Madame Weigel's pattern business was started by Polish-Australian woman Johanna Weigel. They sold a million patterns in 1915 alone.

Intermediate

Peplum blouse

Start the summer in great style. The relaxed fit and softly bloused top with its peplum is very smart.

The Australian Women's Weekly, 15 December 1971.

Materials: 10-ply crochet cotton, 50 g balls: 4 x main colour (MC), 2 x contrast colour (CC); 3.00, 3.50 and 4.00 mm crochet hooks.

Measurements: To fit 100cm bust; length from shoulder 60 cm. Each motif measures 8 cm across.

MOTIFS

With 3.50 mm hook and CC, make 5 ch, sl-st to 1 ch to form a circle.

1st round: 1 ch, work 12 dc into circle, sl-st to 1st dc and fasten off.

2nd round: Join in MC to any dc, 1 dc in same dc, (10 ch, 1 dc in next dc), rep to last dc, 10 ch, sl-st to 1st dc and fasten off.

3rd round: Join in MC to 5th ch of a loop, 1 dc in next ch, (3 ch, 1 dc in next loop) rep to last loop, 3 ch, sl-st to 1st dc.

4th round: Sl-st to 2nd ch of 3 ch sp, 1 ch, 1 dc in same sp, (3 ch, 1 dc in next ch sp) twice, * (3 ch, 1 dc in same sp as last dc) twice (this makes corner), (3 ch, 1 dc in next ch sp) 3 times. Rep from * twice, (3 ch, 1 dc in same sp as last dc) twice, 2 ch, sl-st to 1 dc and fasten off. Make 76 motifs.

TO MAKE UP

To join 2 motifs: With wrong sides of motifs tog, using 3.50 mm hook and MC, join in yarn to 2nd 3 ch loop of a corner of 1st motif, 3 ch, 1 tr in corresponding loop on 2nd motif, (2 ch, 1 tr in next loop on 1st motif, 1 tr in next loop on 2nd motif) 4 times and fasten off. Join motifs in horizontal strips as shown in diagram on page 40.

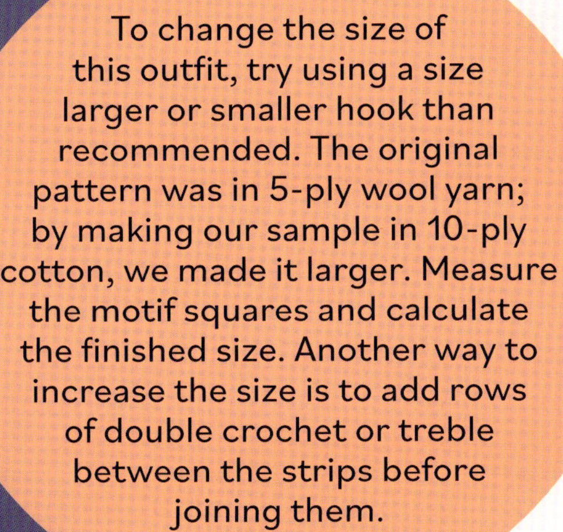

To change the size of this outfit, try using a size larger or smaller hook than recommended. The original pattern was in 5-ply wool yarn; by making our sample in 10-ply cotton, we made it larger. Measure the motif squares and calculate the finished size. Another way to increase the size is to add rows of double crochet or treble between the strips before joining them.

We tested and updated the top of this playsuit. Use Trove to find the original pattern to make the matching shorts.

To join 2 strips: With wrong sides of strips tog, using 3.50 mm hook and MC, join in yarn to corner 3 ch loop of 1st motif on 1st strip, 3 ch, 1 tr in corresponding loop on 2nd strip, (2 ch, 1 tr in next loop on 1st strip, 1 tr in next loop on 2nd strip) 4 times to corner, * 2 ch, 1 tr in 3 ch of 3 ch of join of 1st strip, 1 tr in top of last tr of join on 2nd strip, (2 ch, 1 tr in next loop on 1st strip, 1 tr in next loop on 2nd strip) 5 times. Rep from * to end. Cont join strips as shown in diagram, then join A to A for side seam, B to B and C to C for shoulder seams.
Lightly press work on wrong side.

NECK EDGING

With 3.00 mm hook and MC, join in yarn at a back corner, 1 ch, work 1 dc in each loop to end, omitting 1 loop at each join, sl-st to 1st dc.
Next round: (2 ch, 1 dc in next dc) rep to end and fasten off.
Work 2 rounds in each armhole in same way.

LOWER EDGING

With 3.50 mm hook and MC, join in yarn at a side loop, 1 ch, work 1 dc in each loop to end, sl-st to 1st dc.
Next round: (3 ch, 1 dc in next dc) rep to end and fasten off.

TIE

With 4 strands of CC and 4.00 mm hook, make a chain 130 cm long. Thread through join between 1st and 2nd strips of motif joined. Make a tassel from the yarn tails at each end of the tie.

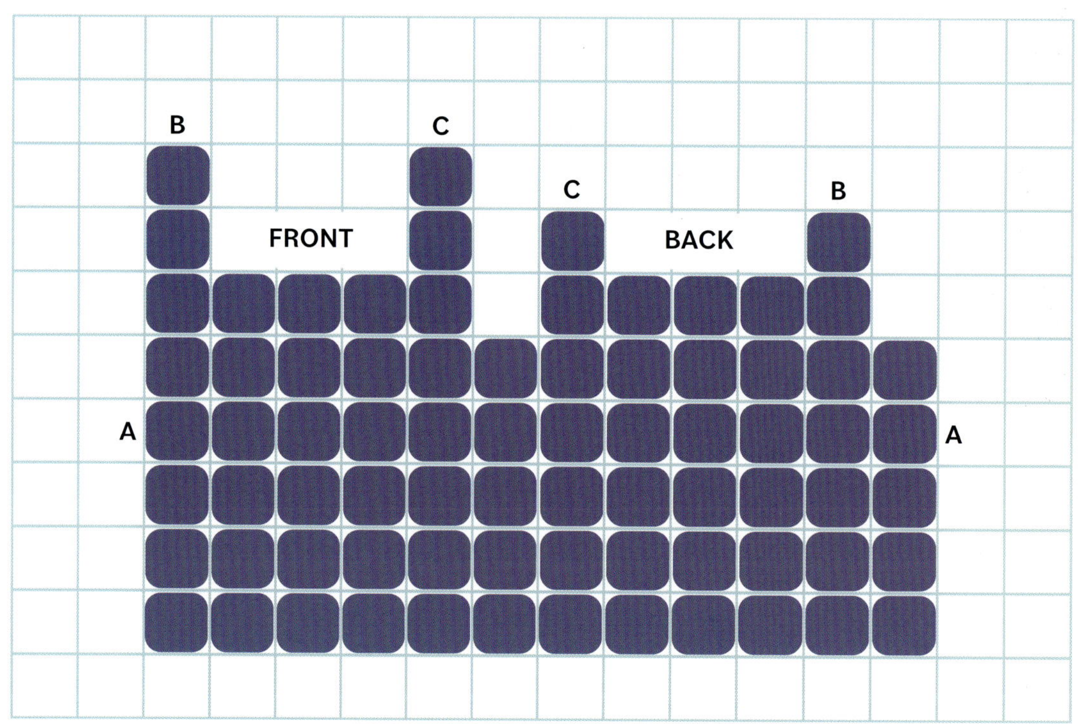

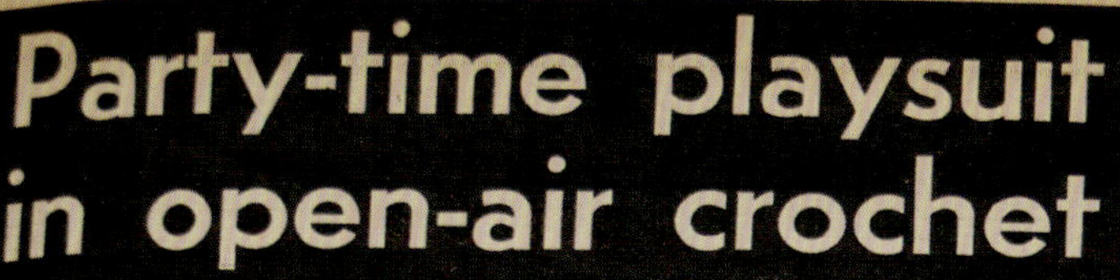

Party-time playsuit in open-air crochet

● This eye-catching playsuit will start you summerwards in great style. The relaxed fit and softly bloused top with its peplum is very new and smart.

Designed by ***JAN OF VILLAWOOL***

— 7 balls
2 balls
Pants
balls

ch., 1 tr. in corresponding loop on 2nd motif, (2 ch., 1 tr. in next loop on 1st motif, 1 tr. in next loop on 2nd motif) 4 times and fasten off.

in motifs in horizontal as shown in diagram.

in 2 strips: With wrong strips tog., using and m.c., join 3 ch. loop strip, 3 ding

Tie: With 4 strands of c.c. and 4mm hook, make a chain 50in. long. Thread through join between 1st and 2nd strips of motifs joined. Make 2 tassels and attach to each end of tie.

PANTS

MOTIF B: Make 12 motifs with 3mm hook, 24 with 3.50mm hook, and 14 with 4mm hook.

With hook and c.c., make 5 ch., sl-st. to 1st ch. to form a circle. Work 1st and 2nd rnds. as motif A. Join in c. and work 3rd and 4th as motif A.

in motifs: Following with c.c. and same as motifs being in motifs into strips as for Top. size as 1st join strips . Join A right of

ide. work rnd. leg as

ght side 3.50mm to a join ch., work 1 loop to end, of 2 ch. 2 ch., 1 d.c. in end, sl-st. to 2nd

d. 5 times and Cut elastic to and attach to waistband, using -st. for casing.

made with 4mm hook

tif made with 3.5 mm (No. 9) hook

Z: with (No. 10)

LEFT LEG

This mod bonnet might not be your thing, but the flower motifs are very quick and easy to make and can be joined together easily to make a bedspread, a blanket, a bag or anything you like.

Beginner

Flower bonnet

If you know anything about crochet, you can make these flower motifs.

The Australian Women's Weekly, 19 April 1967.

Materials: 8-ply yarn, 50 g balls: 1 x main colour (MC), 1 x contrast colour (CC); 3.25 and 4.50 mm crochet hooks.
Measurements: To fit average head. Each motif measures 8 cm square.

MOTIF

Using MC and 3.25 mm crochet hook, work 6 ch, sl-st to form a ring.
1st round: 3 ch, 14 tr into ring, sl-st into top of 3 ch.
2nd round: 1 dc into same sp as sl-st, * 5 ch, miss 2 tr, dc into next sp, rep from * 3 times, 6 ch, sl-st into 1st dc (5 loops). Change colour but do not break off MC.
3rd round: Using CC, * into 5 ch loop work (sl-st into loop, 3 ch, 1 tr, 3 dtr, 1 tr, 3 ch, sl-st into loop), rep from * 4 times. Break off CC and fasten ends.
4th round: Pick up MC, 3 ch, dc into top of 1st tr, 3 ch, miss 1 dtr, dc into next dtr, 3 ch, dc into next tr, 3 ch, dc between petals, rep all round. Fasten off.
Make 11 motifs.

TO MAKE UP

Use a head form or an old hat with a round crown as a base to assemble the motifs. Pin motifs in cap shape, using 7 motifs round sides and back and 4 at top centre. With MC and 3.25 mm crochet hook, join motifs with criss-cross of ch in all sps between petals, working approximately 3 ch to cross a sp. Where petals touch, join with sl-st. Remove base.
Tie fasteners (make 2): Using double strand of CC and 4.50 mm crochet hook, work 60 ch, fasten off. Stitch securely to flower motif at either side of bonnet.

HEAD-LINES for winter

● If you know anything about knitting or crochet, you can make up these smart little headpieces — the perfect accessories for your winter gear. The striped cap at right even has a bag to match.

PEAKED BALACLAVA (above) is buttoned underneath the chin. Directions are below.

CAP AND BAG set (above) are crocheted in wavy stripes. The cap, made in one piece, is finished off with a looped pompon.

PEAKED BALACLAVA

Materials: 3 balls Patons Mayfair yarn; 1 pair No. 8 knitting needles; 3 small buttons.

Measurements: To fit average head, 22in. all round.

Tension: 11½ sts. to 2in., 11 rows to 1½in.

LEFT CHINSTRAP

Cast on 18 sts. Work 8 rows g-st.

9th Row: Inc. 1 st., work to last 4 sts., turn.

10th Row: Sl. first st., k to end.

11th Row: Inc. 1 st., k to last 8 sts., turn.

12th Row: As 10th row.

13th and 14th Rows: Knit.

Rep. rows 9 to 14 once. K 12 rows without shaping.

Next Row: Inc. 1 st. in first and last sts. K 3 rows.

Rep. last 4 rows 3 times more * and sl. sts. on to spare needle.

RIGHT CHINSTRAP

Cast on 18 sts., work 4 rows g-st.

Buttonhole Row: K 2, w.fwd., k 2 tog., k 5, w.fwd., k 2 tog., k 4, w.fwd., k 2 tog., k 1.

K 4 rows without shaping, then rep. from row 9 as for left chinstrap to *. Cont. thus:

Next Row: Cast on 3 sts., k across all sts. on needle, cast on 62 sts., k across sts. on spare needle, comm. at shorter (face) edge. Cast on 3 (128 sts. on needle.) K 14 rows.

Next Row: K 1, k 2 tog., (k 6, k 2 tog.) 15 times, k to end. K 13 rows without shaping.

Next Row: K 1, k 2 tog., (k 5, k 2 tog.) 15 times, k to end. K 10 rows.

Next Row: K 1, k 2 tog., (k 4, k 2 tog.) 15 times, k to end. K 7 rows.

Next Row: K 1, k 2 tog., (k 3, k 2 tog.) 15 times, k to end. Rep. last 8 rows 3 times more, knitting 2 and 1 sts. respectively between k 2 tog. on 1st and 2nd rep., then k 2 tog. 16 times on 3rd rep. K 4 rows.

Next Row: * K 1, k 2 tog., rep. from * to end. K 2 rows.

Run end of yarn through sts. and fasten off. Sew up back seam. Stitch 3 buttons opposite buttonholes.

STRIPED CAP AND BAG SET

Materials: **Hat** — 2 balls each grey, gold, black Patons Jet; **Bag:** 2 balls each grey, gold, black (same wool); No. 6 crochet hook; 8in. frame for bag.

Measurements: Hat, to fit average head.

Abbreviations: Sp., work st. into front of loop only.

Note: Use wool double throughout.

HAT

Using grey, comm. with 27 ch.

1st Row: Sl-st. into second ch. from hook and into next 9 ch., 2 d.c. into next ch., d.c. into next 7 ch., ½ d.c. into next 2 ch., w.o.n. and complete d.c., d.c. into last 6 ch., 2 ch., turn.

2nd Row: 16 d.c., 10 sl-sts.

Join in black, drop grey, 1 ch.

When changing colors, leave loop of approx. 4in. These loops will form pompon at top of hat.

3rd Row: Sl-st. into 10 sps., 2 d.c. into next sp., d.c. into next 7 sps., ½ d.c. into next 2 sps., w.o.n. and complete d.c., d.c. into last 6 sps., 2 ch., turn.

4th Row: As 2nd.

Drop black, join in gold, 1 ch. Rep. 3rd and 4th rows.

These 6 rows form patt.

Cont. working until 7 complete stripe patts. worked.

To Finish: Stitch back seam with black, run a draw thread round top, and fasten securely. Run in all ends.

BAG

Comm. with black, using wool double. Make 15 ch.

1st Row: D.c. into second ch. from hook, d.c. into next 5 sps., ½ d.c. into next 2 sps., w.o.n. and complete d.c., 6 d.c., 2 ch., turn.

2nd Row: 13 d.c. Drop black, join in gold.

3rd Row: 7 ch., d.c. into 2nd ch. from hook, d.c. into next 10 sps., ½ d.c. into next 2 sps., and complete d.c., d.c. into next 5 sps. and into turning ch., 6 ch.

4th Row: 23 d.c. Drop gold, join in grey.

5th Row: 9 ch., d.c. into 2nd ch. from hook, 2 d.c. into next sps., 16 d.c., ½ d.c. into next 2 sps. and complete d.c., d.c. into 10 sps. and into turning ch., 10 ch., turn.

6th Row: D.c. into 3rd ch. from hook, and into each sp. along row. Drop grey, rejoin black.

7th Row: 2 ch., d.c. in first sp., 2 d.c. in next sp., 15 d.c., (½ d.c. into next 2 sts. and complete d.c.) twice, 15 d.c., 2 d.c. into next sp., 1 d.c., 2 ch., turn.

8th Row: 38 d.c. Drop black, rejoin gold. Rep. 7th and 8th rows.

Work 3 reps. of stripe patt., 1 more grey stripe, and a short gold and black strip to correspond with other side.

Fasten off, run in all loose ends. Fold piece in half, and stitch sides to suit bag frame. Stitch bag to frame.

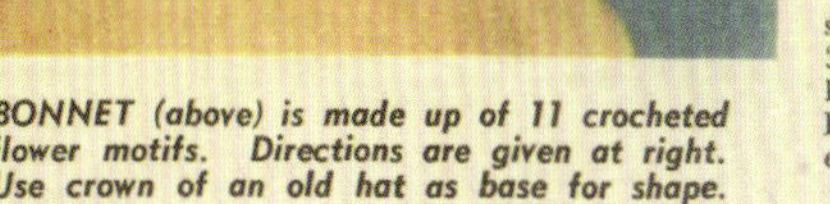

BONNET (above) is made up of 11 crocheted flower motifs. Directions are given at right. Use crown of an old hat as base for shape.

FLOWER MOTIF BONNET

Materials: 1 ball each Patons Courtelle Yarn in navy and white; Milwards Phantom crochet hooks Nos. **7 and 10.**

Measurements: To fit average head.

FLOWER MOTIF

Using navy and No. 10 crochet hook, work 6 ch., sl-st. to form a ring.

1st Round: 3 ch., 14 tr. into ring, sl-st. into top of 3 ch.

2nd Round: 1 d.c. into same sp. as sl-st., * 5 ch., miss 2 tr., d.c. into next sp., rep. from * 3 times, 5 ch., sl-st. into first d.c. (5 loops). Drop navy.

3rd Round: Using white, * into 5 ch. loop work (sl-st. into loop, 3 ch., 1 tr., 3 d.tr., 1 tr., 3 ch., sl-st. into loop), rep. from * 4 times. Break off white and fasten ends.

4th Round: Pick up navy, 3 ch., d.c. into top of first tr., 3 ch., miss 1 d.tr., d.c. into next d.tr., 3 ch., d.c. into next tr., 3 ch., d.c. between petals, rep. all round. Fasten off.

Work 11 motifs.

TO MAKE UP

Use an old felt hat with a round crown for a base to assemble the motifs. Pin motifs to hat base in cap shape, using 7 motifs round head and 4 at top-centre. With navy and No. 10 crochet hook, join motifs with criss-cross of ch. in all spaces between petals, working approximately 3 ch. to cross a space. Where petals touch, join with sl-st. Remove felt base.

Tie Fasteners (Make 2): Using double strand of white and No. 7 crochet hook, work 60 ch., fasten off. Stitch securely to flower motif at either side of bonnet.

Garments

Crochet was not often used for garments until well into the twentieth century, but when the craze for crochet hit in the sixties and seventies there were all kinds of wild and woolly creations as a result.

As an alternative to knitting, crochet has the advantage of easily creating an open, lacy fabric. Crocheted mesh can be more trans-seasonal than knitwear, and even summer items such as a bikini (page 58) can be crocheted.

That doesn't mean winter clothing is out of the question; the coat on page 48 is cosy and cuddly in cluster stitch, and the pattern even includes instructions for a matching pillbox hat.

Crochet is for everyone; we have included two unisex vests (pages 52 and 72) but patterns can be modified to suit the wearer's tastes. For instance, the bikini cover-up (page 62) could be shortened and made into a cool sleeveless top.

Experienced

Winter coat

The symbol of winter chic, this cosy coat has a matching pillbox hat to complete the ensemble.

The Australian Women's Weekly, 15 December 1971.

Materials: 10-ply yarn (40% wool, 40% acrylic, 40% alpaca), 20 (21, 22) x 50 g balls—this includes sufficient yarn for the hat; 5.00 mm crochet hook; fabric for lining, if desired.
Measurements: Pattern in small (medium, large) sizes; length from top of shoulder 100 (100, 102) cm; sleeve seam 43 cm.
Tension: Working in pattern, 3 clusters measure 4.5 cm in width.
Special stitches: Cluster: * yoh, insert hook into next st, draw up a loop approximately 2 cm in length, rep from * 3 times, yoh and draw through all loops.

COAT

BACK

Make 107 (113, 119) ch (including 4 ch to turn).
1st row: yoh, insert hook into 5th ch and make * 1 cluster, 2 ch, miss 2 ch, rep from * to end, ending with 1 cluster, 4 ch to turn—35 (37, 39) clusters.
2nd row: 1 cluster in 1st sp, 2 ch, rep to end of row, 1 cluster in turning ch, 4 ch, turn.
Rep 2nd row until back measures 77.5 cm (or length required).
To shape armholes: Sl-st to 3rd sp from turn, work in patt to last 2 clusters, turn.
Note: When decreasing at beginning of row, turning cluster is not counted.
Dec 1 cluster at each end of next row—29 (31, 33) clusters. Cont straight until armholes measure 23 (23, 24.5) cm.
To shape shoulders: Sl-st over 3 (4, 4) clusters, work to last 3 (4, 4) clusters, turn.
Sl-st over 3 clusters, work to last 3 clusters, turn, rep last row once. Fasten off.

LEFT FRONT

Make 62 (65, 68) ch, including 4 ch to turn and work in patt as given for back—20 (21, 22) clusters—until front measures 77.5 cm or length required.

The pattern is in three sizes and the sizing is generous as the weight of the yarn tends to cause the fabric to stretch. Check your tension regularly as you work and if you are petite consider using a smaller hook size to obtain the desired result.

The original yarn was a 12-ply, but we obtained the correct tension with a 10-ply yarn. Lining with fabric is optional but may help the coat retain its shape without stretching.

To shape armholes: Sl-st to 3rd sp from turn, work in patt to end of row, turn. Dec 1 cluster at armhole edge in next 2 rows—16 (17, 18) clusters.
Cont straight until armhole measures 15 (15, 16.5) cm, ending at front edge.
To shape neck: Sl-st over 2 clusters, work to end of row.
Dec 2 clusters at neck edge in every row until 9 (10, 10) clusters remain.
Note: In the medium size there will be 3 decs of 2 clusters and 1 dec of 1 cluster.
When armhole measures same as back armhole, shape shoulder.
1st row (armhole edge): Sl-st over 3 (4, 4) clusters, work to end of row.
2nd row: Work to last 3 clusters, turn.
3rd row: Sl-st to end of row. Fasten off.

RIGHT FRONT

Work to correspond with left front, reversing all shapings.

SLEEVES

Make 59 (59, 62) ch and work in patt—19 (19, 20) clusters. Inc 1 cluster at each end of every following 4th row until there are 27 (27, 28) clusters.
Cont straight until sleeve measures 36 cm.
To shape top of sleeve: Sl-st over 2 clusters, work to last 2 clusters, turn. Dec 2 clusters at each end of every row 3 more times, then 1 cluster each end twice—7 (7, 8) clusters. Fasten off.
Note: If you wish to use a fabric lining, cut it out now using the crocheted pieces as templates before you join them together.
Make two.

FRONT BANDS

Make 14 ch. Work in dc until long enough to fit along front to neck edge. Fasten off.
Make two.

NECKBAND

Join shoulder seams. Sew front bands in position, fold in half and sl-st in position on wrong side. With right side of work facing, join in yarn at front edge (where band was folded) and work in dc round neck edge to left-front band—work 2 dc in each sp, 1 dc in top of each cluster. Work 14 rows of dc and fasten off.

SLEEVE BANDS

With right side of work facing, join in yarn and work 2 dc in each sp and 1 dc in each end cluster—38 (38, 40) dc. Work 14 rows of dc.
Fasten off.
Make two.

TO MAKE UP

Set in sleeves. Join side and sleeve seams. Fold neck and sleeve bands in half and sl-st in position on wrong side. If using a lining, sew the lining pieces together at shoulder, sleeve and side seams, and finish the seams as desired. Turn and stitch a hem around all edges. Place the lining inside the coat and sl-st to the inside edge of the front, neck and sleeve bands.

HAT

Make 4 ch and join with a sl-st to form a ring.
1st round: 8 dc in ring (mark end of each round with a coloured thread).
2nd round: 2 dc in each dc of prev round (16 dc).
3rd round: 1 dc in each dc of prev round.
4th round: As 2nd round.
5th and 6th rounds: As 3rd round.
7th round: * 1 dc in 1st dc, 2 dc in next dc, rep from * to end of round.
8th and 9th rounds: As 3rd round.
10th round: * 1 dc in each of 2 dc, 2 dc in next dc, rep from * to end of round.
11th and 12th rounds: As 3rd round (64 dc).
13th round: * 1 cluster in 1st dc, 2 ch, 1 cluster in next dc, 2 ch, miss 1 dc, (1 cluster in next dc, 2 ch, miss 2 dc) 6 times. Rep from * twice, 1 cluster in next dc, 2 ch, 1 dc in 1st sp (25 clusters).
14th round: 1 cluster in same sp, * 2 ch, 1 cluster in next sp, rep from *, ending 2 ch, 1 dc in 1st sp.
Rep 14th round 7 times.

Work 3 rounds of dc, working 3 dc into each sp in last cluster round. Fasten off.

LINING (OPTIONAL)

If you wish to line the hat, cut a circle of lining fabric the same diameter as the hat and a strip of fabric to fit around the side of the hat (plus seam allowances). Sew the short ends of the strip together, then sew around the edge of the circle. Turn and stitch a double hem, then sl-st the lining into the hat around the brim.

Beginner

Striped waistcoat

This pretty tricoloured waistcoat is a most useful adjunct to any wardrobe and can be made by the most amateur worker in crochet. Made in a wool-silk blend, it has a gorgeous lustre.

The Australian Woman's Mirror, 13 November 1928.

Materials: 4-ply 80% merino 20% silk yarn, 100 g balls: 2 x main colour (MC), 2 x each of 2 contrast colours (CC1 and CC2); 2.75 mm crochet hook; 4 buttons.
Measurements: To fit 90–100 cm chest.
Tension: 12 tr and 6 rows to 5 cm.

LOWER WAISTCOAT

The waistcoat is worked in one piece from the lower edge. Make 231 ch for the full width of the cardigan in CC2 worked rather loosely. Counting the 1st 3 ch as 1 tr, work 1 tr into each of the remaining ch. Do not break off the colour but carry it up the side of the work. Begin each row with 3 ch in place of 1st tr. Work 1 tr on each tr of prev row, taking up both loops each time.
Work in the colours * 1 row MC, 1 row CC1, 1 row CC2. Rep from * throughout the cardigan. When there are 15 rows from the beginning (finishing after CC2), work the pockets.

POCKETS

First make the two linings as follows: make 33 ch in CC2 and work 1 tr into each ch, taking the 1st 3 ch as 1 tr, making 30 st in all. Repeat in the colours as before until there are 15 rows, then go back to the work and continue as follows:
Next row: 20 tr, miss the next 30 sts and work across the pocket lining instead, then 129 tr into next 129 sts, miss next 30 sts and work across the other lining instead, then 20 tr on remaining 20 sts.
After this continue as before until there are 43 cm (51 rows) from the beg, finishing after a CC1 row.

ARMHOLES AND FRONT SLOPES

1st row: Take 1st 2 tr tog as one, 47 tr, take next 3 trs tog as one, turn.
2nd row: Dec 2 (as above) at beg of the row and 1 at end.

The boyish styles worn by flappers and their ilk in the 1920s make this waistcoat ideal as a unisex garment; a casual wardrobe addition for a cooler day. Easily size up or down by adding or subtracting stitches and rows, or going up or down a hook size.

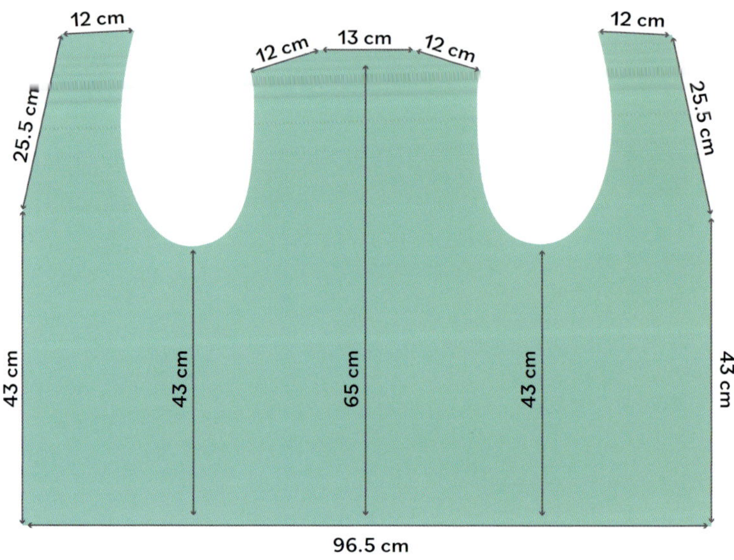

3rd row: Dec 2 at end.
4th row: As 2nd row.
5th row: Dec 1 at end.
6th and 7th rows: Dec 1 at each end.
8th row: Dec 1 at beg of row.
9th row: As 6th row.
10th row: As 8th row.
11th and 12th rows: As 6th row.
13th row: Without dec.
14th row: As 5th row.
15th row: Without dec.
16th row: As 5th row.
17th row: Dec 1 at beg and inc 1 at end.
18th row: 1 tr in each st.
19th row: As 17th row.
20th row: 1 tr in each st.
21st row: As 17th row.
22nd row: Inc 1 at beg and dec 1 at end.
23rd row: Inc 1 at end.
24th row: Inc 1 at beg.
There should now be 28 sts, finishing after a CC1 row.

SHAPE SHOULDERS

1st row: 23 tr, 2 htr, 2 dc, 1 sl-st.
Next row: Miss 1st 7 of prev row, 1 sl-st, 2 dc, 2 htr, 16 tr to the end.
Next row: 9 tr, 2 htr, 2 dc, 1 sl-st.
Next row: Miss 1st 7 of prev row, 1 sl-st, 2 dc, 2 htr, 2 tr. This completes one front.
Go back to where the front was started, miss 10 tr, then take next 2 tog, 101 tr, take next 2 tog, turn. Now dec 1 tr at each end of the next 10 rows, leaving 83 sts; cont without decreasing until there are 21 rows from beg of armhole.
Shape shoulders thus: 1 sl-st, 2 dc, 2 htr, work tr until 5 remain, 2 htr, 2 dc, 1 sl-st.
Next row: Miss 1st 7 of prev row, 1 sl-st, 2 dc, 2 htr, work until 12 remain, 2 htr, 2 dc, 1 sl-st. Rep last row twice more to complete back.
Go back to last full row and miss next 10 trs, take next 3 tog as one, 47 tr, take last 2 tog as one.
2nd row: Dec 1 at beg and 2 at end (as above).
3rd row: Dec 2 at beg.
4th row: As 2nd row.
5th row: Dec 1 at beg.
6th and 7th rows: Dec 1 at each end.
8th row: Dec 1 at end.
9th row: As 6th row.
10th row: As 8th row.
11th and 12th rows: As 6th row.

Crochet Waistcoat
pleted Waistcoat.
out dec.
at beginning and inc
ginning and dec
sts, finishing

13th row: 1 tr in each st.
14th row: As 5th row.
15th row: 1 tr in each st.
16th row: As 5th row.
17th row: Inc 1 at beg and dec 1 at end.
18th row: 1 tr in each st.
19th row: As 17th row.
20th row: 1 tr in each st.
21st row: As 17th row.
22nd row: Dec 1 at beg and inc 1 at end.
23rd row: Inc 1 at beg.
24th row: Inc 1 at end.
Shape shoulder thus:
1 sl-st, 2 dc, 2 htr, 23 tr.
Next row: 16 tr, 2 htr, 2 dc, 1 sl-st.
Next row: Miss 1st 7 of prev row, 1 sl-st, 2 dc, 2 htr, 9 tr.
Next row: 2 tr, 2 htr, 2 dc, 1 sl-st.

TO MAKE UP

Press the work on both sides with a warm iron over a damp cloth. Sew up shoulder seams and sew pocket linings into place. With MC, work a row of dc round each armhole, then a row of tr and a row of dc, decreasing 1st every now and then to shape the armhole. Next work a row of dc all round the edges of waistcoat, then a row of tr, a row of dc, a row of tr, and a row of dc, putting 3 into each corner st to make the corners lie flat. When working the 2nd row of dc, work four buttonholes up the front at regular intervals as follows: 4 ch, miss 4 tr of prev row.

In next row work 4 tr over the 4 ch.

Across each pocket top work a row of dc, a row of tr and a row of dc. Press seams and edges and sew buttons on left front to correspond with the buttonholes on the right.

Artificially made

Alex Woolner's AI narwhal, left, and 'Norma the Normal Fish' at right. As Norma's bulbous brown eyes suggest, these were both based on patterns from ChatGPT.

AI's ability to invent crochet patterns is a fascinating intersection of technology and traditional craftsmanship. Leveraging vast datasets and machine learning algorithms, AI demonstrates a capacity to analyse existing patterns, identify patterns within patterns, and suggest novel combinations that might elude human designers.

This computational creativity can lead to the generation of innovative crochet patterns, offering fresh perspectives and pushing the boundaries of what is conventionally achievable. However, the challenge lies in maintaining the art's inherent warmth and personal touch, as crochet is not only about stitches and colours but also about the tactile experience and emotional connection that arises from human creativity. Striking a delicate balance between AI-driven innovation and the irreplaceable human touch is key to harnessing the full potential of technology in the world of crochet pattern design.

This is ChatGPT's response to a query on the ability of artificial intelligence programs to generate patterns. Although it acknowledges its own shortcomings, it fails to mention some of the other problems that have emerged as crocheters have tested these new technologies.

When ChatGPT launched in late 2022, crocheters were among the many who flocked to test the system's potential to generate patterns. They were often disappointed with the results: a giraffe with no neck and enormous ears; a narwhal with a single fin, bulging eyes and a large bulbous tusk pointing vertically from its head. These certainly weren't the first failed trials. In 2019, an American research scientist worked on teaching a neural network to create crochet hat patterns; HAT3000 generated coral-looking ruffles and even a pattern with the instruction 'toss the pieces together'.

There are ways for technology to assist crocheters, including apps that let you pull together from a bank of existing patterns and data to change sizes, for example. Inventing patterns altogether, however, still requires a human touch. Unfortunately, this doesn't stop unscrupulous online retailers using AI-generated images of supposed crocheted objects to sell fake patterns. Keep an eye out for crocheted objects that are too perfect, stitches that just seem to disappear or unbelievable colours.

Intermediate

Bikini

The smartest beach gear on this year's summer scene.

The Australian Women's Weekly, 15 December 1971.

Materials: 4-ply (fingering) cotton yarn, 4 x 50 g balls; 3.00 mm crochet hook; round elastic, approximately 1 m.
Measurements: To fit 86 (92, 96.5) cm bust.
Tension: 12 tr and 6 rows to 5 cm over tr.
Special stitches: Dec: (yoh, draw up a loop in next st, yoh and draw through 2 loops) twice, yoh and draw through 3 loops; inc: 2 tr in next st.

PANTS FRONT

Make 13 ch.
1st row: Miss 3 ch, 1 tr in next ch, 1 ch, miss 1 ch, 1 tr in each of next 5 ch, 1 ch, miss 1 ch, 1 tr in each of last 2 ch. **
2nd row: (1 dc, 1 ch) in 1st tr, 1 tr in each of next 4 sts, 1 ch, miss 1 tr, 1 tr in each of last 5 sts.
3rd row: (1 dc, 1 ch) in 1st tr, 1 tr in next tr, 1 ch, miss 1 tr, 1 tr in each of next 5 sts, 1 ch, miss 1 tr, 1 tr in each of last 2 sts, rep 2nd and 3rd rows once, then 2nd row once. Inc twice at each end of every row until there are 59 (67, 75) sts.
Join in another ball to beg of last row and make 14 (13, 12) ch. Fasten off.
Return to main work and make 16 (15, 14) ch, miss 3 ch, patt to end.
Join in another ball to beg of last row and make 42 ch. Fasten off.
Return to main work and make 43 ch, miss 1 ch, 1 dc in each st to end. Work 1 row dc. Fasten off.

PANTS BACK

Work as front to **. Inc at each end of every row until there are 45 sts. Inc twice at each end of next row. Inc at each end of next row. Rep last 2 rows until there are 87 (93, 99) sts.
Join in another ball to beg of last row and make 42 ch. Fasten off.
Return to main work and make 43 ch, miss 1 ch, 1 dc in each st to end. Work 1 row dc. Fasten off.

This bikini is worked in a tiny block pattern with a shell border. Pants are tied at the sides.

TO MAKE UP

Using a flat seam, join crotch seam. Work 1 row dc around leg and waist edges, working over elastic.

Next row: 1 ch, 1 dc in next dc, * miss 2 dc, 5 tr in next dc, rep from * to end. Fasten off.

BIKINI TOP (MAKE 2 PIECES)

Make 43 (49, 55) ch

1st row: Miss 3 ch, 1 tr in next ch, * 1 ch, miss 1 ch, 1 tr in each of next 5 ch, rep from * to last 3 ch, 1 ch, miss 1 ch, 1 tr in each of last 2 ch.

2nd row: (1 dc, 1 ch) in 1st tr, * 1 tr in each of next 4 sts, 1 ch, miss 1 tr, 1 tr in next st, rep from * to last 4 sts, 1 tr in each of next 4 sts.

3rd row: (1 dc, 1 ch) in 1st tr, 1 tr in next tr, * 1 ch, miss 1 tr, 1 tr in last 2 sts. Dec twice at each end of next row. Dec at each end of next row. Rep last 2 rows until 5 sts remain.

Next row: (1 dc, 1 ch) in 1st tr, (yoh, draw up a loop in next st, yoh and draw through 2 loops) 4 times, yoh and draw through 5 loops, make 100 ch. Fasten off.

Make 100 ch and attach to end of 1st row for one piece and to the beg of the 1st row for 2nd piece.

TO MAKE UP

Work 1 row dc evenly around all edges, then 1 ch, 1 dc in next dc, * miss 2 dc, 5 tr in next dc, miss 2 dc, 1 dc in next dc, rep from * around neck edge and neck side of neck straps only. Fasten off. Catch 2 pieces tog at centre front and gather up.

The original pattern also contains instructions for a cover-up and a beach bag. Check the pattern on Trove for details.

Flight of the
Sasha Grishin
Vintage

Beginner

Bikini cover-up

This see-through shift to slip on over your swimsuit for picnics and barbecues at the beach is easy to crochet. It can be made with or without sleeves; if you like the no-sleeve look, work the neck edging round the armholes, too.

The Australian Women's Weekly, 13 November 1968.

Materials: 6-ply (sport) cotton-bamboo yarn, 11 (12, 13) x 50 g balls—for a sleeveless dress; 3.50 and 3.25 mm crochet hooks; 2 stitch markers (optional).
Measurements: To fit 86 cm bust; length 93 cm; sleeve 45 cm (if using 5-ply wool as in the original pattern, fits 96.5 cm bust). Adjust by adding or subtracting 6 ch for each size in the foundation row.
Tension: 1 patt to 3 cm.

BACK

Using 3.50 mm hook, make 120 ch.
Foundation row: 1 dc into 9th ch from hook, * 6 ch, miss 5 ch, 1 dc in next ch, rep from * to 3 ch from end, 3 ch, 1 dtr in last ch, turn.
1st row: 2 ch, insert stitch marker if using, 4 dc into 1st loop, * 4 ch, 1 dc into 3rd ch from hook to make picot, 9 dc into next loop, rep from * to end, finishing with 5 dc in last loop, turn.
2nd row: 2 ch, insert stitch marker if using, 6 ch, * 1 dc in 5th of next 9 dc, 6 ch, rep from * to end, remove stitch marker from prev row, 1 dc, turn.
3rd row: 2 ch, insert stitch marker, 9 dc into 1st loop, * 1 picot, 9 dc into next loop, rep from * to end, remove stitch marker from prev row, 1 dc, turn.
4th row: 2 ch, insert stitch marker, 4 ch, * 1 dc in 5th of 9 dc, 6 ch, rep from * to end, 3 ch, remove stitch marker, 1 dtr, turn.
Rep these 4 patt rows until work measures 35 cm, ending on row 4 (always measure work when it is hanging).
Dec for waist as follows:
** **Dec row 1:** As 1st patt row.
Dec row 2: 2 ch, insert stitch marker, 5 ch, * 1 dc in 5th of 9 dc, 5 ch, rep from * to end, remove stitch marker, 1 dc, turn.
Dec row 3: As 3rd patt row.

The original garment was made in 5-ply wool; we have modernised it in 6-ply cotton-bamboo. The use of cotton instead of wool makes the dress smaller, but the size can easily be adjusted by adding six chains (one pattern) in the foundation row for each size; for example, adding six chains will make the back and front of the dress 3 cm larger, therefore the finished dress will be 6 cm (one size) larger.

Our crocheter also recommends using stitch markers to ensure the work stays straight.

Dec row 4: 2 ch, insert stitch marker, 4 ch, * 1 dc in 5th of 9 dc, 5 ch, rep from * to end, 3 ch, remove stitch marker, 1 dtr, turn. **
Rep these 4 rows. Now work a 2nd round of dec as follows:
2nd dec row 1: As 1st patt row, ending with 3 dc in last loop. Remove stitch marker, 1 dc, turn.
2nd dec row 2: 2 ch, insert stitch marker, 4 ch, * 1 dc in 5th of 9 dc, 5 ch, rep from * to last loop of prev row, 4 ch, remove stitch marker, 1 dc, turn.
2nd dec row 3: As 3rd patt row, ending with 8 dc in last loop, remove stitch marker, 1 dc, turn.
2nd dec row 4: 2 ch, insert stitch marker, 3 ch, * 1 dc in 5th of 9 dc, 5 ch, rep from * to last loop of prev row, 2 ch, remove stitch marker, 1 dtr, turn.
Rep 2nd dec rows 1–4 until work measures 60–70 cm, ending on a 3rd row. Fasten off.

TO SHAPE ARMHOLES

Next row: *** Rejoin yarn to 4th dc of 1st 9 dc, 1 dc in same dc, * 5 ch, 1 dc in 5th of 9 dc, rep from * to end, ending at centre of last 9 dc, turn.
Next row: As 3rd patt row.
Next row: Sl-st to 5th dc, 1 dc in this dc, * 5 ch, 1 dc in 5th dc, rep from * to end, ending at centre of last 9 dc, turn. ***
Repeat these last 2 rows until work has decreased to 13 patts.
Work one 4th patt row and then cont in patt until armholes measure 18 cm, ending on a 3rd patt row.

TO SHAPE NECK

Next row: **** 2 ch, insert stitch marker, 4 ch, (1 dc in 5th dc, 5 ch) twice, 1 dc in 5th dc, 5 ch, 1 dtr, turn.
Next row: As 3rd patt row, ending with 4 dc in final loop.
Next row: 2 ch, insert stitch marker, 4 ch, (1 dc in 5th dc, 5 ch) twice, 1 dc in 5th dc, turn.
Next row: 2 ch, (9 dc in next loop) twice, remove stitch marker, 1 dc. Do not make picots in this row. Fasten off.
2nd side of neck: Rejoin yarn to 5th dc of 3rd 9 dc group from armhole edge. Work 1 dc in this dc, (5 ch, 1 dc in 5th dc) twice, 5 ch, 1 dc in last dc of prev row, turn.
Next row: 4 dc in 1st loop, then as 3rd patt row.
Next row: Sl-st to 5th dc, 1 dc, 5 ch, 1 dc in 5th dc, 5 ch, 1 dtr, turn.
Next row: 2 ch, (9 dc in 1st loop, 1 dc) twice.
Do not make picots in the row. Fasten off. ****

FRONT

Work as back until armholes measure 14 cm (dec to 12 loops).
To shape neck: Work as back neck shaping from **** to ****, working 8 patt rows more on each shoulder after the shaping is completed.

SLEEVES (OPTIONAL)

With 3.25 mm hook, make 84 ch. Work in patt as back for 18 cm, ending with a 3rd patt row.
Now repeat the 4 dec patt rows (from ** to **) until sleeve measures 41 cm, ending on a 1st patt row.
To shape top: Work as given for armhole shaping of back from *** to ***, then rep the last 2 rows 5 times.
Next row: As 3rd patt row, omitting the picots.

TO MAKE UP

Lightly press. Join shoulder seams, sew in sleeves if using, join side and sleeve seams.

NECK EDGING

Join yarn to shoulder seam. With 3.25 mm hook, beg with 3 ch, work 1 row of tr all round, working a sl-st into top of each picot and 4 tr between the picots, ending with 1 sl-st into top of 3 ch.
Next round: 4 ch, * miss 1 tr, 1 tr in next tr, 1 ch, rep from * to end, sl-st into top of 3rd chain.
Next round: With 3.50 mm hook, work 3 ch, 1 tr in 1st ch sp, * 2 tr in next ch sp, rep from * to end, sl-st into top of 3 ch. Fasten off.
Work sleeve and lower edge borders the same, but use 3.25 mm hook for last round. Press all seams and edgings.

BIKINI COVER-UP
See-through shift to slip on over your swimsuit for picnics and barbecues at the beach is easy to crochet. It can be made with or without sleeves; if you like the no-sleeve look, work the neck edging round the armholes, too. Directions are below.
To Shape Neck: Work as back neck shaping from **** to ****, working 8 patt. rows more on each shoulder after the shaping is completed.
SLEEVES
With No. 9 hook, make 72 (78, 84) ch. Work in patt. as back for 7in., ending 4th patt. row.
Now repeat the 4 dec. patt. rows (from ** to **) until sleeve measures 16½in.,

Intermediate

Striped singlet top

A crochet top that can be worn two ways in bright sunny colours will make an attractive addition to a summer wardrobe. Wear it with shorts, pants or as a bikini cover-up for going to and from the beach.

The Australian Women's Weekly, 15 December 1971.

Materials: 6-ply (sport) cotton yarn, 50 g balls: 3 x main colour (MC), 1 x each of 3 contrast colours (CC1, CC2 and CC3), 1 x dividing colour (DivC); 3.00 and 3.50 mm crochet hooks; 1 mm millinery elastic.

Measurement: Can be made to fit any desired bust size.

Tension: 5 sts to 2.5 cm on 3.50 hook; 12 rows (6 rows tr and 6 rows dc) to 10 cm.

Special abbreviations: fl, front loop; bl, back loop.

FRONT CENTRE PANEL

Using 3.50 mm hook and MC, make 50 ch.

1st row: 1 dc in 2nd ch from hook, 1 dc in each ch to end, 1 ch, turn—48 dc.

2nd row: Picking up fl only, 1 dc in each dc to end, 3 ch, turn.

3rd row: Picking up bl only, miss 1 dc, 1 tr in each dc and turning ch, 3 ch, turn.

4th row: Picking up fl only, miss 1 tr, 1 tr in each tr, and top of turning ch, 1 ch, turn.

5th row: Picking up bl only, 1 dc in each tr to end, 1 ch, turn.

6th row: Picking up fl only, 1 dc in each dc to end, 3 ch, turn.

Rows 3 to 6 form pattern. Work in patt until 33 rows have been worked. Work 1 row dc around outer edges, working 46 on each side and 3 dc in each corner st. With right side facing, join DivC at lower edge corner. Picking up bl of each dc, 1 dc in each dc to top corner, turn. Drop DivC, join in CC1.

Next row: 3 ch, fl only, 1 tr in each dc to end, 3 ch, turn.

Next row: Bl only, 1 tr in each tr to end, turn. Drop CC1.

Next row: Using DivC, 1 ch, fl only, 1 dc in each tr to end, 1 ch, turn.

Straps are crocheted in a combination of the colours used in the stripes. Our crocheter found that the top band tightened the fit somewhat, so be generous with the size and perhaps consider going up a hook size for the top band.

The front panel is the same for all sizes, and you simply crochet as many stripes at the back as you need for your measurements.

Next row: Bl only, 1 dc in each dc to end, turn. Drop DivC.
Repeat last 4 rows to form pattern. Continue in patt, working 2 tr rows in each of CC1, CC2 and CC3 with 2 rows dc using DivC between each stripe, until you reach the desired bust measurement, ending with 1 row dc in DivC. Stitch to opposite side of centre panel using a sl-st seam worked in the front loop of the front panel. Darn in ends. Using 3.00 mm hook, work 1 row dc across top and lower edges of striped section, using matching colours.

TOP BAND

Using MC and 3.50 mm hook, with right side facing, join yarn in 3rd DivC strip. Bl only, work 1 row dc across 2 stripes, top edge of centre panel and corresponding stripes on other side. Cut cotton. Work 2 more rows in dc across top edge beginning and ending with 1 stripe extra on each side. Do not cut yarn on 3rd row, but continue in dc around entire top edge. Work 3 more rows in dc, working in bl only and working over hat elastic on last 2 rows.
Cut cotton. Fasten off.

LOWER BAND

Using MC and 3.50 mm hook, with right side facing, join yarn at side of centre square. Work 4 rows dc, picking up bl only. Fasten off.

DAISY CHAIN STRAPS

Using DivC, make 4 ch, join with sl-st to form ring.
1st round: 1 ch, 11 dc in ring, join with sl-st, drop DivC and join in CC1.
2nd round: 3 ch, 1 tr in same st, 2 tr in each st to end, join in top of 3 ch with sl-st. Cut yarn, leaving a long tail for sewing together.
Make 6 daisies in each of 3 colours. Join 9 tog for each strap and stitch in place.

Crochet on display

In the 1970s, Australian galleries, from Shepparton Art Gallery in regional Victoria to the National Gallery in Canberra, were reappraising their existing acquisition policies and adding decorative arts to their collections. A landmark exhibition at the start of the decade at the National Gallery of Victoria, LANDFALL, included examples of textiles and homewares. In the exhibition catalogue, the curator writes:

> *One of the most rewarding aspects of working on LANDFALL has been in juxtaposing the decorative arts and support material against the paintings and sculptures which are their more widely known contemporaries. It is this pursuit in particular which might well be elaborated in future projects ...*

The magazine *Craft Australia* was launched a year later. Its second edition, published in December 1971, included a profile of Ewa Pachucka. Pachucka was a crochet artist who created works on a sculptural scale in soft fibres: 'She turned away from weaving because, for her, it was too slow and limiting. Now she uses only a simple crochet hook, and works with natural fibres of sisal, jute, millet and hemp'. Born in Poland, she exhibited internationally in America and Europe before emigrating to Australia, where she spent almost thirty years in Sydney and Tasmania. Her work stands out in the collections of international galleries because she used humble materials and what was traditionally seen as a very domestic women's craft to create grand works of art.

In that same *Craft Australia* edition, the editorial opens with the declaration that 'The craft movement gains momentum in Australia at a rate we would scarcely have dreamed of ten years ago'.

Left: Ewa Pachucka, *Arcadia: Landscape and figures* (detail); above: Frances (Budden) Phoenix, *Get your abortion laws off our bodies* (see page 27); below: Trevor Smith, *Pig's head platter*.

Throughout the decade, 'soft sculpture' and textile courses were added to existing training courses and commercial galleries dedicated entirely to decorative arts were established. The Australian National Gallery, as it was then called, appointed a Curator of Australian Decorative Arts in 1980, and was gifted approximately 750 objects collected by the Crafts Board of the Australia Council in the same year.

More recently, some crochet artists have leaned into crochet's domesticity. In 2022, the Art Gallery of Ballarat hosted an exhibition of South Australian artist Trevor Smith that included a tableau of a dinner party, crocheted in wool. A crocheted pig's head, its mouth stuffed with a bright red crocheted apple, sits on top of a platter of crocheted vegetables; roast turkey and a beautifully decorated fruit cake complete the meal. Explaining Smith's work, the gallery writes that 'his quirky and inventive crochet sculptures stem from his interest in costume, characters, fashion, culture and history and push the boundaries of crochet in a move from functional items to creative artworks'.

The original pattern appears to have been designed for a teenager but with a little ingenuity you can upsize it. To increase the chest size, add one repeat of the arrowhead pattern to each side when you are working the shoulders.

Alternatively, you could work more or fewer dc rows between the arrowhead rows. To increase the length, add multiples of four chains (one arrowhead or 1.5 cm) to the foundation chain. If you wish to save time and yarn, the back may be worked in dc only, using the front piece as a template for the shaping.

Experienced

Arrowhead vest

The arrowheads on this sharp-looking pullover are quite simple to create. You'll master the special technique faster than you can string your bow.

The Australian Woman's Mirror, 15 September 1948.

Materials: 4-ply machine-washable wool yarn, 8 x 50 g balls; 2.50 mm crochet hook.
Measurements: To fit chest 90 cm; length 62 cm.
Tension: 6.5 arrowheads and 17 pattern rows to 10 cm.
Special stitches: Double cross stitch (DCS):
* yoh, insert needle at base of the 4th tr back along work, draw the thread through loosely, yoh and draw through all loops on needle.
Rep from *. This makes one side of the arrowhead patt.

THE FRONT

Commence with 91 ch (waistband to underarm).
1st row: 90 dc into 90 ch, turn with 1 ch.
2nd row: 90 dc, 3 ch, turn (this 3 ch in 1st tr in each tr row).
Note: Our crocheter preferred to work 2 ch and not count it as the 1st stitch of the row.
3rd row: 4 tr on 4 dc, * 1 DCS, 4 tr on next 4 dc.
Rep from *, ending with 2 tr on 2 dc.
4th row: 2 tr on 2 tr, * 4 tr on 4 tr, 1 DCS, inserting the hook exactly on top of the DCS of prev row, forming the arrowhead of the patt. Rep from * to end. (This is now the armhole end).
Work 6 rows of dc, inc 1 dc at armhole end in each row.
11th row: 2 tr on 2 dc, * 4 tr on 4 dc, 1 DCS.
Rep from *, ending with 2 tr on 2 dc.
12th row: 2 tr on 2 tr, * 4 tr on 4 tr, 1 DCS.
Rep from *, ending 2 tr on 2 tr, inc 2 tr, 1 DCS.
The last DCS has no corresponding half.
Work 6 rows of dc, inc 2 dc at armhole end in each row.
Work 20 ch for armhole.
Keeping the continuity of patt, work the next 10 rows without further inc.

Shape neck by sl st over 8 tr of next row, then dec 1 st at neck edge of each of the following 21 rows, keeping in patt.
Work 1 row of arrowhead patt.
This is now the centre front.
Now work the other side to correspond, working from centre front to side and reversing the shapings.

THE BACK

Work exactly as for the front until the neck shaping is reached.
Shape back neck by dec 1 st at neck edge on each of the next 6 rows, then work without further dec to the centre back.
Complete the other side to correspond as for the front.

THE WAISTBAND

Work 16 rounds of dc, drawing in work slightly to the desired waist measurement.

THE ARM BANDS

Work 8 rounds of dc.

THE NECK BAND

Work 8 rounds of dc, dec 1 st at centre front in every round.

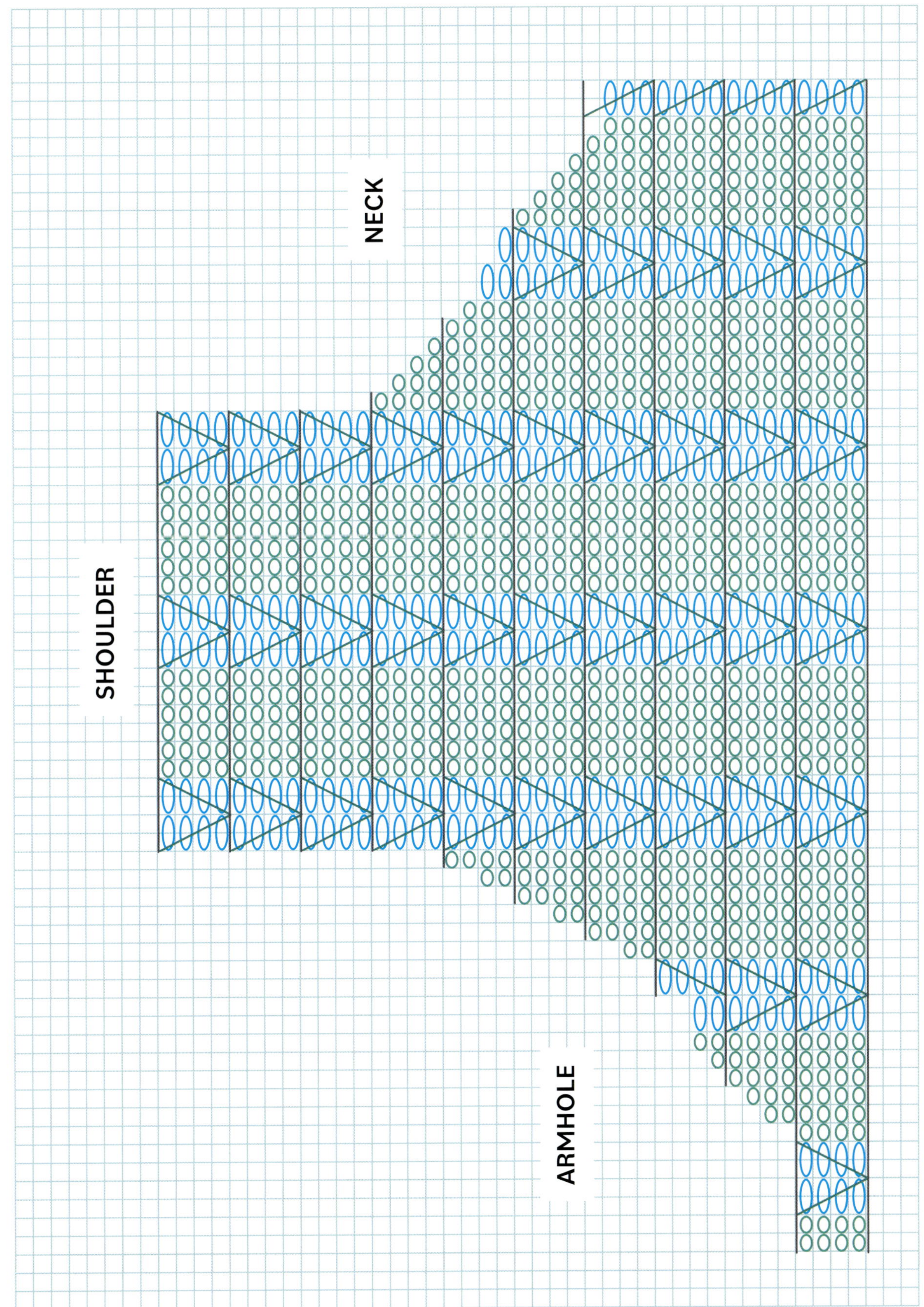
NECK
SHOULDER
ARMHOLE

Intermediate

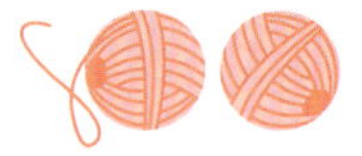

Rainbow cardigan

This light-hearted jacket for off-duty hours was made from scraps of yarn highlighted with vividly rich and deeper toned yarns.

The Australian Women's Weekly, 20 May 1944.

Materials: 4-ply acrylic yarn, 50 g balls: 1 x main colour (MC) for borders, 6 or 7 x various colours or scraps of 4-ply acrylic yarn from your stash; 3.00 mm crochet hook.

Measurements: To fit 84 cm bust. To increase the size, simply add 2 ch (1 tr square) for each extra centimetre across the back and fronts. You may also need to adjust the armhole and sleeve sizes. Alternatively, work in 5- or 6-ply yarn with a larger crochet hook to obtain a larger size over all.

Note: For the fronts, sleeves and pockets, each colour was commenced 3 squares from the beginning of the row and finished 3 squares from the beginning of the next row; thus, each colour was used for one row at a time. In the back of the jacket, each colour was carried 12 squares into each row.

THE BACK

Make ch of 96, work 1 tr into 5th ch, then 2 ch and 1 tr into 2nd chain from prev tr. Continue across row (45 tr).

Commence each row with 5 ch (instead of 1 tr and 2 ch), then 1 tr into the top of every tr of prev row, with 2 ch between each tr. Continue until work measures 36 cm (repeating colours regularly).

Miss 6 squares at each side for armhole shaping.

Miss 1 square at each end of next 3 rows, then continue straight until work measures 51 cm.

Work 2 rows on 8 squares of each side of work for shoulders.

FRONTS (BOTH ALIKE)

Commence with 42 ch (20 squares) and work until piece measures 36 cm.

Miss 8 squares for armhole.

When work measures 46 cm, miss 4 squares at neck edge.

When work measures 53.5 cm, finish off.

This pattern is a great way to use up small amounts of leftover yarn without the result looking too piecemeal.

In the original garment, pastel colours were arranged in groups, with darker colours between the groupings. Colours were joined by crocheting the last 7.5 cm of colour just finished and first 7.5 cm of new colour together for one treble stitch, and the ends were cut off when each piece of the garment was completed.

was knitted in a very attractive
e with regard to color, but please
directions to success.

jacket in

for off-duty
s of pastel-
vividly rich
ols.

f jacket each color was
squares into each row.

THE BACK

in of 96, work one treble
in, then 2 chain and one
2nd chain from previous
ontinue across row (45

e each row with
stead of 1 treble
n), then one
the top of every
h of pre-
with 2 chain
each
ntinue
meas-
inches
regular
colors
quares at

2nd Row: K 1, * p 4, k 1, repeat from * to end.

Repeat last 2 rows.

5th Row: P 1, * sl. 2 sts. on a spare needle and leave in front of work, k 2, k the 2 sts. from spare needle, p 1, repeat from * to end.

6th Row: Repeat 2nd row.

Repeat last 6 rows for 8in. Change to No. 10 needles and repeat 1st and 2nd rows only. When work measures 12in. shape armholes by casting off 5 sts. at the beginning of the next 2 rows. K 2 tog. each end of the next 5 rows, then every 2nd row 5 times. When armholes measure 2in. work the 6 rows of cable pattern, commencing with the 5th row. When armholes measure 4in. work as follows: Work 46 sts. (leave remaining 40 sts. on spare needle). Continue on last 46 sts. and when armhole measures 7in. shape shoulder by casting off 10 sts. at armhole edge every 2nd row 3 times. Cast off. Join wool at centre-back, cast on 6 sts., work to end of row. Work to correspond with other side.

Continued on page 29

THIS JACKET was designed to fit sizes 32 and 33. If you are an expert with the crochet hook, however, you can make it in any size to suit yourself.

SLEEVES

Make 60 ch and work 30 tr as for back. When work measures 12 cm, miss 1 square at each end of next 3 rows. Work straight until sleeve measures 36 cm.
Make two.

POCKETS

Make 30 ch and work 15 tr as for back.
Work 14 rows.
Make two.

TO MAKE UP

Join shoulder seams and side seams.
Sew up sleeves and set in, taking a big pleat in the fullness at top of sleeve.
With MC yarn, work 2 rows dc around each pocket piece and sew on pockets.

BORDERS

Work 8 rows dc round cuffs.
Work 12 rows dc right around edges, front and neck of garment, inc around corners at centre front and dec around corners in neckline.
Work 6 more rows of dc down each front edge.
Press well with damp cloth.

We found the sleeves quite narrow. Check the fit and add extra stitches if they are too tight. The extra fabric can be taken in to the pleat at the top of the shoulder when the sleeves are attached.

Beginner

Poncho skirt

In sprightly stripes, this is a jaunty addition to any wardrobe of smart casuals.

The Australian Women's Weekly, 15 December 1971.

Materials: 8-ply merino yarn, 50 g balls: 13 x main colour (MC), 3 x 1st contrast colour (CC1), 8 (9) x 2nd contrast colour (CC2), 7 x 3rd contrast colour (CC3); 4.00 mm crochet hook; 15 cm skirt zipper; approx. 2 m round elastic.
Measurements: To fit 86 (92) cm hips; waist, 61 (66) cm; length (at side edge), 66 cm.
Tension: 14 sts to 7.5 cm and 18 rows to 13 cm over patt.

BACK AND FRONT

Work begins at waist. Using CC1, make 62 (68) ch.
1st row: Using CC, miss 1 ch, 1 dc in each of next 30 (33) ch, 2 dc in next ch, 1 dc in each ch to end.
2nd row: Using CC2, 3 ch, 1 tr in each of next 30 (33) dc, 2 tr in next dc, 1 tr in each dc to end.
3rd row: Using CC2, 3 ch, 1 tr in each of next 31 (34) sps, 2 tr in next sp, 1 tr in each sp to end.
4th row: Using CC3, 1 ch, 1 dc in each of next 31 (34) sps, 2 dc in next sp, 1 dc in each sp to end.
5th row: Using CC3, 1 ch, 1 dc in each of next 32 (35) dc, 2 dc in next dc, 1 dc in each dc to end.
6th row: As 5th row.
7th row: Using MC, 3 ch, 1 tr in each of next 33 (36) dc, 2 tr in next dc, 1 tr in each dc to end.
8th row: Using MC, 3 ch, 1 tr in each of next 33 (36) sps, 2 tr in next sp, 1 tr in each sp to end.
9th row: Using MC, 3 ch, 1 tr in each of next 34 (37) sps, 2 tr in next sp, 1 tr in each sp to end.
10th row: Using CC1, 1 ch, 1 dc in each of next 34 (37) sps, 2 dc in next sp, 1 dc in each sp to end.
Rows 2 to 10 form patt. Cont in patt, inc in centre of every row (as before) until side edge measures 63.5 cm.
Fasten off.
Repeat for other side.

WAISTBAND

Using a flat seam, join side seams, leaving 12 cm open at top of left seam.
Using MC, work 7 rows dc evenly along waist, missing 2 dc at lowest point of front and back and working last 3 rows over elastic, drawing elastic up to keep work firm. Fasten off.
Sew in zipper.
Using doubled yarn in MC, crochet a chain about 150 cm long to use as a tie, if desired.

FOR AUTUMN

● It's the season to be merry – in the gayest, most carefree knits you ever knew. This collection of swinging casuals features the new shapings, the new colors. Make them yourself in jet time, and wear on all the fun-filled days.

Directions for making on pages 32 and 33

DESIGNS BY
HEATHER DOBSON

VEST or jacket, call it what you will, is a cute style to wear on many occasions. You knit it in easy stocking-stitch, add the flourish of contrast diamonds in felt pieces. Edges have a crochet loop trim.

PONCHO SKIRT, in sprightly stripes, is a jaunty addition to any wardrobe of smart casuals. This one is crocheted in two pieces, starting from the waist, so that you can go to the length you like the most. (Below the knee is smartest, we say.) Bonus pattern: a snug crocheted cap.

Accessories

Scarves, gloves, bags and hats in crochet are quick and easy projects. In this section, you'll also see how some unusual materials can be used to crochet everyday items.

Wool and cotton yarn are the obvious choices for crocheted garments because of their flexibility and absorbency, but in this part of the book you might want to consider other materials that can be used to make items more durable or interesting to look at. For example, we've used a raffia-style material for the pochette (page 94); you can buy this rayon paper craft yarn or you could also use natural raffia, though it is a little more difficult to work with.

In the past there has been a trend to use strips cut from plastic bags, such as bread bags as a material to crochet into accessories such as hats, bags and even clothing. This is another option you can explore; for example, a plastic bag yarn might make the shopping carry-all (page 108) even more durable, helping you bring home the bacon in style!

Our mod collars (page 98) are worked in fine crochet cotton, but you could also try these designs in lurex threads and other decorative options for different effects.

Beginner

Mesh scarf

A scarf is a quick and easy project that is a great way to use up odd balls of yarn. This loopy lace design means that multiple colours can be easily combined.

The Australian Woman's Mirror, 15 July 1953.

Materials: 4-ply machine-washable 100% wool yarn, 50 g balls: 1 x each of 6 colours or 600 g in total; 3.00 mm crochet hook.
Measurements: 38 cm wide x 150 cm long.
Tension: Each mesh measures about 2 cm.
Foundation row: Make 87 ch loosely.
1st row: 1 dc into 11th ch from hook, * 5 ch, miss 3 ch of foundation, 1 dc into next ch. Rep from * to end. Break off yarn, leaving an inch or two to run in afterwards and draw through stitch on hook to fasten off firmly.
2nd row: With next colour, make a slip loop on the hook and work 1 dc into 1st dc, 5 ch, 1 dc into 1st loop, * 5 ch, dc into next loop. Rep from * to end. Break off yarn and fasten off as for 1st row.
Rep the 2nd row throughout, changing colour for each row.
Last row: Work 3 ch instead of 5 between each dc, to correspond with foundation edge.

TO FINISH

Darn in ends neatly. Make a fringe along each end as follows: Cut 15 cm lengths of wool in all colours, using 6 strands at a time (1 of each colour), fold in half, draw the loop through the 1st loop at one end, then draw the ends through the loop and pull tight. Rep for each end loop of the scarf.

The original scarf used six colours of wool yarn, but you can vary the colour scheme with as many or as few colours as you like.

To keep the edges of the scarf straight as you work, pull the dc to the centre of each loop in the row below after you finish crocheting each row.

The pattern for these gloves is in three sizes, made in No. 8 pearl cotton. Using 2-ply crochet cotton gives a thicker and less stretchy fabric, so go up a size if you choose this. Measure your work against your hand regularly to check the fit, especially if you have long fingers.

We made the gloves plain, without the embroidery and beads. If you can't get fil à dentelles cotton, you could use a single or double strand of embroidery cotton for the embroidery instead.

Intermediate

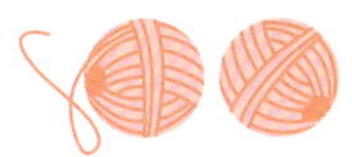

Cotton gloves

Quickly and easily made, these crocheted gloves are smart and cool for summer wear.

The Australian Women's Weekly, 4 February 1953.

Materials: No. 8 pearl cotton, 4 (5, 5) x 10 g balls; 1 ball fil à dentelles lace crochet cotton (if using); 20 small glass beads (if using); 2 mm crochet hook, 1.25 mm crochet hook for flowers (if using).
Measurements: To fit small (medium, large).
Tension: 5 dc and 4 ch sps to 2.5 cm, 8 rows to 2.5 cm.
Special stitches: Inc: 1 dc, 1 ch, 1 dc in same ch sp; Dec: (insert hook in next ch sp, yoh, draw loop through) twice, yoh and draw through all loops on hook.

LEFT GLOVE

BACK OF HAND

Starting at little finger side with no. 8 cotton, chain 67 (73, 79) sts.
Note: The chain will seem too long at first, but the following rows will pull it up to an appropriate length.
1st row: Dc in 3rd ch from hook, * ch 1, skip next ch, dc in next ch, rep from * to end, ch 2, turn.
2nd row: Skip 1st dc, * dc in next ch sp, ch 1, skip next dc, rep from * to end, ending with dc in last sp, ch 2, turn.
The 2nd row establishes the patt.
Working in patt throughout, inc 1 dc at tip of finger on 3rd row and dec 1 dc at tip of finger on 5th row.
Cont in patt until 6 rows in all have been made. Work is at wrist edge.
Ring finger: Work across to last 9 (10, 11) sps. Chain 25 (27, 29) sts.
Next row: As 1st row.
Work in pattern over these sts for 7 rows, inc 1 dc at tip of finger on 2nd row and dec 1 dc at tip of finger on 6th row.
Middle finger: Work across to last 11 (12,13) sps, ch 27 (29, 31) sts. Work as for ring finger.
Index finger: Work across to last 12 (13, 14) sps, ch 25 (27, 29) sts. Work as for ring finger.
Break off yarn.

PALM

Starting at little finger side, work as for back of hand until middle finger has been completed. Work in at wrist edge.

FRONT OF THUMB

Work in patt over the next 17 (18, 19) sps, then ch 23 (25, 27) sts. Turn.

Next row: Dc in 3rd ch from hook, * ch 1, skip next ch, dc in next ch, rep from * across ch sts, cont in patt, across next 17 (18, 19) sps.

Working over these sts only as for ring finger, inc 1 dc at end of 2nd row, ch 2, turn.

3rd row: Work in patt to within 6th sp from wrist edge, sl-st in next sp, turn.

4th row: Work in patt to end.

5th row: Cont in patt, working to wrist edge until 9 rows have been completed, dec 1 dc at tip of thumb on 8th row. Break off yarn.

BACK OF THUMB AND INDEX FINGER

Attach thread to starting chain at tip of thumb. Work in pattern across starting chain of thumb, to within 12 (13, 14) sps, from tip of middle finger, ch 25 (27, 29) sts.

Next row: Dc in 3rd ch from hook, ch 1, and cont in pattern across chain and across thumb, ch 2, turn. Work 6 more rows as before over these sts only, inc and dec as before at tips of both thumb and index finger.

Work 1 more row across thumb. Break off yarn.

For medium size, work 1 row of dc around edges of all fingers on back of hand.

For large size, work 1 row of dc around edges of all fingers on back of hand and on palm. Press pieces through a damp cloth. Sew palm and back pieces together, leaving wrist edge open. Sew thumb seam.

Note: We finished each glove with a row of dc around the wrist edge, rather than using the contrasting fil à dentelles.

RIGHT GLOVE

Work same as for left glove, reversing pieces when joining.

EMBROIDERY (OPTIONAL)

Make 20 flowers. Starting at centre with fil à dentelles and using 1.25 mm hook, 5 ch, 2 dtr in 5th ch from hook, 4 ch, dc in same place, (4 ch, 2 dtr in same place, 4 ch, dc in same place) 3 times. Break off. Using fil à dentelles doubled and starting at tip of each finger, embroider 1 row of stem stitch along centre row of each finger on back of hand, ending at wrist edge.

Do not embroider thumb. Sew flowers onto stripes, spacing them alternately with a bead in the centre of each. Using fil à dentelles doubled, dc closely around wrist edge with 2.00 mm hook.

Using recycled materials

Marjorie Bligh was well known to many Australians as Tasmania's 'domestic goddess' and 'housewife superstar', famous for her advice over the years on gardening, cooking, house management, crafts (such as crochet and knitting) and, sometimes, relationships.

Her celebrity as 'queen of the household scene' started with her newspaper columns in the 1950s and grew to encompass six advice books on a range of topics. However, she is perhaps most well-known for her efforts and interest in reusing and upcycling household waste to create knitted and crochet garments, homewares, toys and so much more. Bligh was a pioneer recycler and abhorred the growing waste of a throwaway society. She transformed thousands of used stockings, plastic shopping bags and chicken-feed bags into hats, vests, slippers and other items—wearables and homewares—saving them from going to landfill. In 1986, at the State Country Women's Association Handcraft Exhibition, she won an award in the thrift section for a tablecloth she had made using 314 pairs of stockings, cut in a spiral and crocheted into granny squares.

In 2019 and 2020, after Bligh's passing, Launceston's Queen Victoria Museum and Art Gallery honoured her with an exhibition and with an installation that resulted in the largest community project QVMAG had seen. Members of the public donated old yarn, washed stockings and plastic to QVMAG for *Yarn bombing for Marjorie* in an effort to cover the yellow poles at the entrance to the museum for the exhibition *Marjorie Bligh: Domestic goddess*, which showcased her life and accomplishments.

Bligh was not the only one using thrifty recycling techniques to create something new and upcycled. In the 1970s, multimedia artist Evelyn Roth received international attention for her work, which used repurposed videotapes to construct movable sculptures and garments.

To make her pieces, Roth would use a hammer to crack open a VHS cassette tape and extract the tape from the reels. Using her finger as her crochet hook, she would loop the tape together to make long chains and create innovative structures and wearable garments.

Having moved to Vancouver in the 1960s, Roth began her art focus on knitting and crocheting there, receiving donations of old videotapes from television stations across Canada. A performance in 1972 involved her driving from Vancouver to St. Johns in a car wrapped in a 'snug video cosy',

made of crocheted videotapes. Another, in 1973, draped a 100-foot (30-metre) videotape canopy, made from donated materials from 16 television stations, over the Vancouver Art Gallery's entrance. She was dubbed Canada's 'Recycle Queen' and has now been crocheting recycled materials for over fifty years. Her work has been featured in expos, festivals and exhibitions all over the world.

Now living in South Australia, Roth continues her mission to keep 'TV stations' thousands of miles of unused video tape out of landfill or from being burned into the atmosphere'. She holds workshops on how to crochet strips of tape for practical and community uses, runs programs in schools and continues her artistic practices.

In 2023, there are even more materials you can crochet with to follow in the footsteps of these pioneer recycling crocheters. Plarn, or plastic yarn, is a popular material made from plastic bags, which are cut into strips and joined to make continuous 'yarn'. Various techniques of cutting the bags, such as the slit-skirt method or the spiral method (look them up online if you want to learn more), allow you to cut strips as long as possible to minimise the number of knots required. The resulting long strands can be rolled into a ball and crocheted to make fun projects, such as shopping bags and small baskets. Plarn is a water-resistant non-organic material, and so can be made into sleeping mats in initiatives to help homeless people.

Another extremely popular recycled material is t-shirt yarn. T-shirt yarn can be made using similar methods to plarn and is great for making rugs, baskets, plant hangers and many other projects. It is a good way to recycle old clothing and combat fast fashion.

When trying to find other materials you could potentially recycle and repurpose for your crochet projects, there are a few things to consider. Is the material flexible enough to wrap around a crochet hook or be manoeuvred into loops? Does the material give you strands that are long enough to crochet, or long enough to be looped together to create a continuous strand? And, lastly, is the material durable?

Left: Evelyn Roth, *TV trap*; Right: Roth in *Video armour*, in front of Vancouver Art Gallery in 1973, covered in the videotape canopy.

Beginner

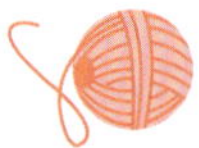

Pochette

This wrap-over purse can be made in the same silk as one's beret or to tone with a frock or coat.

The Australian Woman's Mirror, 17 March 1931.

Materials: Raffia yarn, 40 g balls: 1 x main colour (MC), 1 x each of 2 contrast colours (CC1, CC2); 4.50 mm crochet hook; 18 x 27 cm piece of interfacing and fabric for lining.
Measurements: This original is a small pochette, 17 x 10 cm. If a larger size is required all the measurements given should be increased.
Tension: Not important, simply crochet to the size you want.

POCHETTE

Foundation row: In MC, make 25 ch or to length desired for width of purse.
Every row: Dc into each ch, turn with 1 ch and continue with dc, taking up the front loop only of each st in prev row, turn with 1 ch and continue working in dc until the piece of crochet measures about 22 cm.
Break off yarn and join CC1; continue, making a band about 5 cm wide (work measures 27 cm in total from foundation row).

Note: We used MC for the whole piece and coloured the final section using a Sharpie marker! To do this, roughly colour with the marker then spray with isopropyl alcohol to encourage the marker ink to bleed into the raffia for even coverage.

ROSES

Using CC2, make 4 ch, sl-st to join in a circle.
Small petals: (1 dc, 3 tr) rep 5 times into the ring. Do not break off yarn.
Big petals: (3 ch, sl-st into back post of next dc) rep 5 times, making 5 loops behind the 1st 5 petals. Work 1 dc and 5 tr into each loop. Fasten off, leaving a tail for sewing flowers on to band of pochette.
Make enough roses to fit across the pochette, spacing them as desired.

TO MAKE UP

Press with hot iron over a damp rag on wrong side. This causes the crochet to stretch and

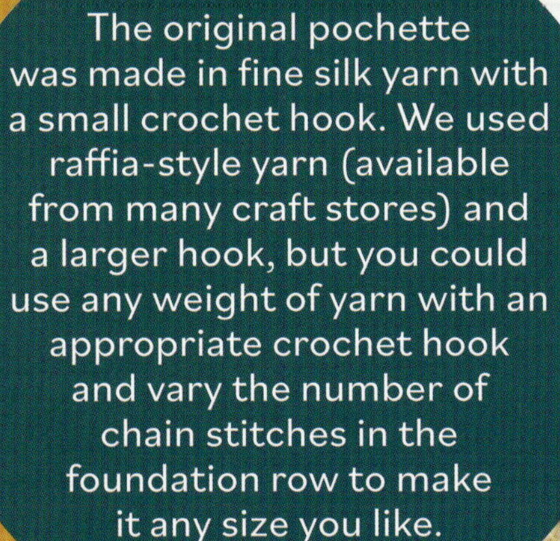

The original pochette was made in fine silk yarn with a small crochet hook. We used raffia-style yarn (available from many craft stores) and a larger hook, but you could use any weight of yarn with an appropriate crochet hook and vary the number of chain stitches in the foundation row to make it any size you like.

If making a larger size in wool or cotton yarn, you might need a stiff lining between the crocheted outer and the inner lining to help it hold its shape.

of each stitch in previous row; turn with 1 ch and continue working in dc until the piece of crochet measures about $9\frac{1}{2}$in. Break off the thread and join on black; continue, making a band about $1\frac{1}{4}$in.

of the crochet background. Bring thread out at point, hold under thumb, put needle in slightly to lower right of point and bring out on centre vein; turn thread to left and hold under thumb, insert needle at left of

The Completed Pochette.

Press with hot iron over damp rag on wrong side. This causes the crochet to stretch and thus prevents further stretching

top and bring out slightly to left of centre vein; repeat on right side, then on left; it will be seen that centre vein can be made

thus prevents further stretching after the bag has been made up. Trim interfacing to slightly smaller than finished crochet piece, then cut lining fabric to same size as crochet piece. Lay the interfacing on the wrong side of the fabric, turn the edges of fabric over the interfacing and lightly tack in place. Pin this lining with wrong sides together to crochet piece and sl-st firmly into position. Now fold into the shape of the pochette, allowing the flap to end about 2 cm from the bottom.

Join the sides of the pochette together using your preferred method. We used dc in the MC raffia. Break off yarn and finish all ends.

Sew roses equidistant along front band, catching back petals down and using your fingers to encourage the small petals to sit up. Embroider leaves and stems if you wish.

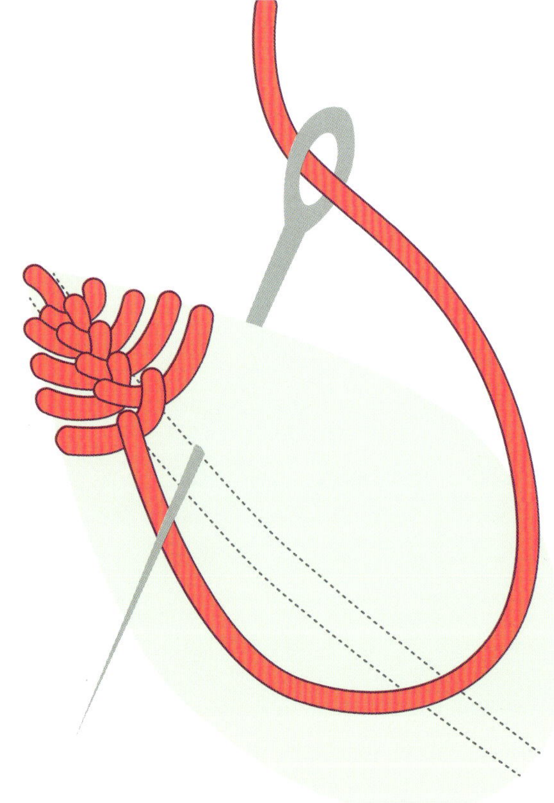

This diagram demonstrates a cretan stitch for the leaves. Stems are chain-stitched, overcasting each link to raise them up.

Crochet in wartime

A Queen's Scarf, awarded to Du Frayer for bravery at Karee Siding on 11 April 1900.

In the collections of the Australian War Memorial is a photo of Private Alfred Du Frayer of the NSW Mounted Rifles, posing with a crocheted scarf draped across his breast like a sash. The scarf was made using double crochet and chain stitch and is one of eight that were handmade by Queen Victoria during the Boer War. The Queen used a deep gold yarn and embellished her scarf with her monogram embroidered in silk.

A useful skill for queens and servicemen alike, crochet has been used in myriad ways in wartime. Horses wore cotton fly veils over their eyes, crocheted by the men of the 3rd Divisional Signal Company in the First World War. Wounded soldiers were taught to crochet as part of their rehabilitation in the Boer War and the First and Second World Wars of the twentieth century. Parcels of crochet wool would be sent out from the rehabilitation stores of the Red Cross to hospitals caring for repatriated servicemen and women. Prisoners of war in Stalag 383, Hohenfels, Germany, crocheted cushion covers to pass the time. Crocheted comforters, scarves, hats and socks sent from home were just as welcome as their knitted counterparts in the cold and wet trenches.

On the home front, crochet designs often featured patriotic sentiments or exhortations for peace. A cotton doily in filet crochet, made during the First World War, shows a woman surrounded by doves carrying olive branches. It bears the message: 'Waiting for the dawn of peace. Lord, bless our brave sailors. We want peace with honour.' Another from 1915 displays flags, a shield and a pine tree and reads: 'Lone Pine. Greater love. Rest in peace.' A doily made in 1979 for the feminist art show The D'oyley Show provides an alternative view. Surrounding a garland of three-dimensional flora and leaves, the message reads: 'Lest we forget the women raped in wars'.

Intermediate

Mod collars

Dress up cool summer shifts and plain tops with these delightful crochet collars and cuffs. As well as making ideal gifts, they give an individual look to off-the-peg dresses.

The Australian Women's Weekly, 10 November 1965.

Materials: 3-ply mercerised crochet cotton (we used DMC Petra size 5), 100 g balls—1 ball of yarn will make multiple collars; 2.00 mm crochet hook; 12 mm pearl shank buttons.
Measurements: Knot-stitch collar 49 cm, cuff 27 cm. Fan design collar 40 cm, front trim 19 cm. Lacy look collar 38 cm. Shell shape collar 36.5 cm, cuffs 24.5 cm.
Special stitches: Knot stitch (ks): draw up 6 mm loop on hook, yoh and pull through, 1 dc in single loop of st.

KNOT-STITCH (BLUE)

Begin with 110 ch.
1st row: 1 dc in 1st ch from hook, 1 dc in each ch to end (109 dc), 2 ch, turn.
2nd row: Miss 1 dc, 1 dc in next dc, * 2 ch, miss 1 dc, 1 dc in next dc, rep from * to end of row, 2 ch, turn.
3rd row: 1 dc in 1st sp * knot stitch (ks), 1 dc in next sp, rep from * to end of row, 4 ch, turn.
4th row: 1 dc in dc, * 4 ch, 1 dc in dc, rep from * to end of row, 2 ch, turn.
5th row: Rep 3rd row, increasing length of ks loop slightly, 5 ch, turn.
6th row: 1 dc in dc, * 5 ch, 1 dc in dc, rep from * to end of row, 3 ch, turn.
7th row: Rep 5th row, increasing length of ks loop slightly.
8th row: Rep 6th row.
9th row: Rep 5th row, loop length should now be about 12 mm, 7 ch, turn.
10th row: * Sl-st in 4th ch from hook to form picot, 3 ch, 1 dc in dc, 7 ch, rep from * to last picot, 3 ch, 1 dc in dc.
Work htr border down ends of collar.
Work a button loop of 7 ch, 7 dc in loop on one end and fasten off. Attach button to other end of collar.
Fasten off.
To make cuffs: Ch 65 and work as for collar.

Collars and cuffs can be temporarily or permanently attached to round necklines and wrist edges of dresses and tops.

FAN DESIGN (PINK/PURPLE)

Make 5 ch, join in circle with sl-st, 2 ch, 7 tr in circle, * 5 ch turn, 1 dc in 3rd tr from hook, 2 ch turn, 7 tr in 5th loop, rep from * 28 times (30 fans).

Make another length of 30 fans.

To join shells: With wrong sides together, proceed as follows: 1 dc in 1st tr of both circles, 2 ch, 1 dc in 1st circle, 2 ch, 1 dc in 2nd circle, * 2 ch, 1 dc in sp between fans of 1st length, 2 ch, 1 dc in sp between fans of 2nd length, rep from * to end of lengths, joining last 2 fans together with sl-st.

Fasten off.

Inside edge of collar: Join yarn to centre of 1st fan, * 2 ch, 1 dc between 1st and 2nd tr of next fan, rep from * to end and fasten off.

Front trim: Make 5 ch, join in circle with sl-st, 2 ch, 7 tr in circle, * 5 ch, turn, 1 dc in 3rd tr from hook, 2 ch, turn, 7 tr in 5 ch loop, rep from * 8 times (10 fans). Proceed thus: 1 ch, * 3 dc in side of tr, 1 dc in sp between fans, rep from * to end, 3 dc in circle, sl-st in 2nd ch, turn, 1 dc in each dc, ending at neck edge. Make a buttonhole loop as for knot-stitch collar.

Fasten off.

LACY LOOK (GREEN)

Begin at outer edge with 11 ch.

1st row: 1 tr in 11th ch from hook, 3 ch, turn.

2nd row: 11 tr in sp, 1 tr in 4th ch made, 1 ch, turn.

3rd row: 1 dc in each tr, 1 dc in top of turning ch (13 dc), 5 ch, turn.

4th row: Miss 1st 2 dc, 1 dc in next dc, * 5 ch, miss 1 dc, 1 dc in next dc, rep from * 3 times

more, 2 ch, miss next dc, 1 tr in next dc, 10 ch, turn.
5th row: 1 dc in 5 ch loop, 3 ch, turn.
6th row: 11 tr in sp, 1 tr in 4th ch of 10 ch counting from the tr below, 1 ch, turn.
Rep 3rd to 6th row until 21 patts have been worked.
Next row: Work 168 dc along straight edge as follows: 4 dc in tr section and 2 dc in loops, 10 ch, turn.
Next row: Miss 7 dc, 1 dc in next dc, * 10 ch, miss 7 ch, 1 dc in next dc, rep from * to end of row, 6 ch, turn.
Next row: 1 dc in 1st loop, * 6 ch, 1 dc in next loop, rep from * to end of row, 2 ch, turn.
Next row: 1 dc in 1st loop, * 5 ch, 1 dc in next loop, rep from * to end of row, 3 ch, turn.
Next row: * 5 tr in loop, 1 dc in dc, rep from * to end of row.

Make a buttonhole loop as for knot-stitch collar. Fasten off.

SHELL SHAPE (YELLOW)

Begin with 109 ch.

1st row: 1 dc, in 1st ch from hook, 1 dc in each ch (108 dc), 3 ch, turn.

2nd row: 1 tr in next dc, * 2 tr in next dc, 1 tr in each of next 2 dc, rep from * to last 8 dc, 2 tr in next dc, 1 tr in each dc to end (142 tr), 3 ch, turn.

3rd row: 1 dc in 3rd tr, * 3 ch, miss 1 tr, 1 dc in next tr, rep from * to end (71 loops), 3 ch, turn.

4th row: 4 tr in 1st loop sp, * 3 ch, miss 1 loop sp, 5 tr in next loop sp, rep from * to end, 3 ch, turn.

5th row: * 1 tr in each of next 2 tr, 2 tr in next tr, 1 tr in each of next 2 tr, 1 ch, 1 tr in sp, 1 ch, rep from * to last tr group, work as other groups, 3 ch, turn.

6th row: * 1 tr in each of next 6 tr, keeping last loop on hook (7 loops in all) yoh and draw through all loops, 3 ch, 1 dc in next sp, 1 dc in next sp, 3 ch, rep from * to last 6 tr, work as 1st 6 tr, 6 ch, turn.

7th row: 1 dc in top st of tr groups, * 6 ch, 1 dc in top st of tr groups, rep from * to end of row, 2 ch, turn.

8th row: 1 tr, 2 ch, 1 tr in sp, 2 ch, 1 dc in dc, * (2 ch, 1 tr, 2 ch, 1 tr) in next sp, 2 ch, 1 dc in dc, rep from * to end of row, 2 ch, turn

9th row: * Into sp between 2 tr of prev row work (1 tr, 1 ch, 1 tr, 1 ch, 1 tr, 3 ch, sl-st in 3rd ch from hook to make picot, 1 ch, 1 tr, 1 ch, 1 tr, 1 ch, 1 tr, 1 ch) 1 tr in dc of prev row, 1 ch, rep from * to last dc, 1 dc.

Make a buttonhole loop as for knot-stitch collar. Fasten off.

To make cuffs:

Ch 59 and work as for collar.

1st row: 58 dc.

2nd row: 74 tr.

3rd row: 37 loops.

We used hessian to line this bag, which gives it a great square shape. If you don't like the idea of this coarse material, you could use canvas or a heavy cotton drill instead.

Beginner

Book bag

Every girl needs something to carry her bits and pieces around in, and not any old bag will do. This one's the grooviest, it's crocheted and lined with sturdy fabric.

The Australian Women's Weekly, 10 June 1970.

Materials: 8-ply machine-washable wool yarn, 50 g balls: 5 x main colour (MC), 3 x each of 2 contrast colours (CC1, CC2); 4.50 mm crochet hook; 50 cm hessian for lining.
Measurements: 36 cm deep, 26 cm wide, 5 cm gusset.
Tension: 9 dc and 11 rows to 5 cm.

FRONT AND BACK

Using MC, make 19 ch loosely.
1st round: Miss 1 ch, 1 dc in each ch to last ch, 4 dc in last ch; working along other side of foundation ch, work 1 dc in each of next 16 ch, 2 dc in next ch, join with a sl-st in ch at beginning of round.
2nd round: Using CC1, 1 ch, 3 dc in next dc (corner dc), 1 dc in each of next 16 dc, 3 dc in next dc (corner dc), 1 dc in each of next 2 dc, 3 dc in next dc (corner dc), 1 dc in each of next 16 dc, 3 dc in next dc (corner dc), 1 dc in next dc, join with a sl-st in ch at beg of round.
3rd round: Using CC2, 1 ch, 1 dc in next dc, 3 dc in next dc (corner), 1 dc in each of next 18 dc, 3 dc in next dc, 1 dc in each of next 4 dc, 3 dc in next dc, 1 dc in each of next 18 dc, 3 dc in next dc, 1 dc in each of next 2 dc, join with a sl-st in ch at beg of round. Cont in dc in stripes of 1 round MC, 1 round CC1, 1 round CC2, working 3 dc in each corner dc in every round until 28 rounds have been worked from beg, thus ending with a round of MC.
Fasten off.
Repeat for other side.

GUSSET

Using MC, make 172 ch loosely.
1st row: Miss 1 ch, 1 dc in each ch to end (171 dc).
2nd row: 1 ch, 1 dc in each dc to end.
Rep 2nd row 9 times.
Fasten off.

STRAPS

Using MC, make 61 ch loosely.

1st row: Miss 1 ch, 1 dc in each ch to end (60 dc).

2nd row: 1 ch, 1 dc in each dc to end.

Rep 2nd row 3 times.

Fasten off.

Repeat for 2nd strap.

TO MAKE UP

Using crocheted pieces as pattern, cut the lining fabric to fit all pieces. Turn in a small hem on the fabric and stitch the lining to the crochet pieces with wrong sides together. Use a flat seam to join the gusset to the front, base and back of the bag, leaving the top open. Sew straps to front and back of bag.

SCHOOL DAZE (left). Every girl needs something to carry her bits and pieces around in, and not any old bag will do. This one's the grooviest, it's crocheted and lined with hessian — all the girls at school want one, too. Directions are overleaf.

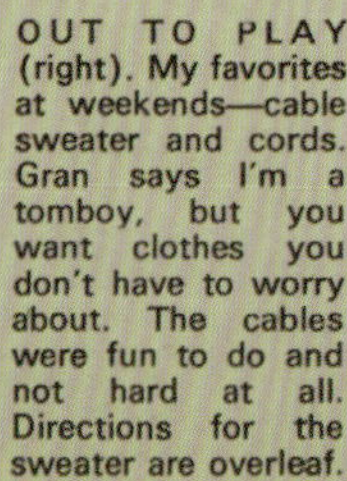

OUT TO PLAY (right). My favorites at weekends—cable sweater and cords. Gran says I'm a tomboy, but you want clothes you don't have to worry about. The cables were fun to do and not hard at all. Directions for the sweater are overleaf.

On show

Rev. David Hughes working on a supper cloth made up of 180 medallions. The whole project took him an estimated 423 hours, or more than 17 days straight.

In 1915, under the headline 'Poor Representation', a *Sun* journalist bemoaned the 'garish', 'tedious' exhibits of needlework on display at Sydney's Royal Easter Show. 'Every year,' they wrote, 'one visits the display of women's work at the Royal Easter Show in the hope that it will be better than in previous years, and every year one comes away disappointed'. It doesn't seem to have occurred to the writer that women might have had other priorities in the second year of the First World War than crocheting for exhibition. The one display that escapes harsh critique is the crocheted lace collars (see ours on page 98), which the writer concedes are 'beautiful, and compare favorably with real Irish crochet'.

Crochet was very much a nascent artform in the first decades of the twentieth century, despite being represented among craft displays in annual agricultural shows. It would reach its first peak in popularity in Australia in the 1940s. As early as March 1940, Judith Cassell, writing for the *Narandera Argus and Riverina Advertiser*, declared herself 'lost in admiration for [her] sex' by what she had seen in the Arts and Crafts pavilion of the Royal Easter Show. She was concerned she might 'run out of adjectives', although she needn't have worried:

> *... and then the crochet! Even in laces it is hard to imagine anything so fine and beautiful. The sort of thing that when you were very young and given to visions you dreamt of queens possessing. One crocheted d'oyley represented balloons of light, and it is quite impossible to attempt to describe the loveliness of the crochet centres in filet designs.*

When men participated in crochet competitions, it was viewed as a novelty. *The Australian Women's Weekly* devoted half a page in 1953 to retired Methodist minister Rev. David Hughes of Cremorne who entered 'three bedspreads, a supper cloth, a bathmat, and two string bags' into the Royal Easter Show. In 1961, an entry in the show by Mr Edwin A. Turner of Ryde made the news under the headline 'Old Man Has Crochet Entry'.

Beginner

Shopping carry-all

There's plenty of space in this expandable shopping bag for your groceries, or a beach towel and all of your picnic paraphernalia.

The Australian Woman's Mirror, 3 January 1951.

Materials: 10-ply cotton yarn, 4 x 100 g balls; 4.50 mm crochet hook.

BASE

Work 20 ch.

1st row: 1 tr into 5th ch from hook (count as 1 sp), * 2 ch, miss 2 ch, 1 tr into next ch. Rep from * to end of row (6 sps).

2nd row: Turn, 5 ch, 1 tr into 1 tr,* 2 ch, 1 tr into next tr. Rep from * to end of row.

3rd to 24th rows: Rep 2nd row.

SIDES

1st row: Into last sp at corner: 15 ch, 1 dc, 15 ch, 1 dc, 15 ch.

Into next sp: 1 dc, 15 ch, 1 dc, 15 ch.

* Into next sp: 1 dc, 15 ch. Rep from * to 22nd sp.

Into 23rd sp: 1 dc, 15 ch, 1 dc, 15 ch.

Into corner sp: 1 dc, 15 ch, 1 dc, 15 ch, 1 dc, 15 ch.

Into next sp: 1 dc, 15 ch, 1 dc, 15 ch.

* Into next sp: 1 dc, 15 ch. Rep from * once more.

Turn the corner in the same manner as the last corner, and rep all around the base of the bag, ending with a sl-st into the same sp as the beg of row.

2nd row: Sl-st to centre of loop of 15 ch, * 15 ch, 1 dc into the centre of next loop. Rep from * all round, ending with sl-st to the centre of the 1st loop of last row.

3rd to 9th rows: Rep 2nd row.

10th row: Sl-st to centre of loop, 8 ch, 1 tr into next loop, * 5 ch, 1 tr into next loop. Rep from * all round, ending in patt.

11th row: Sl-st to centre of bar of 5 ch, 5 ch, 1 tr into next bar, * 2 ch, 1 tr into next bar. Rep from * all round, ending in patt.

Fasten off.

Originally made in red macrame cord, we chose 10-ply cotton to make this oversized version. You could also use a fine hemp twine for a more traditional string bag effect.

Using 4-, 5- or 8-ply yarn and a smaller hook will keep the size of the bag closer to the original dimensions. You can also reduce the number of squares in the base or the number of chain stitches in each loop in the sides. Make the handles as long or short as you like.

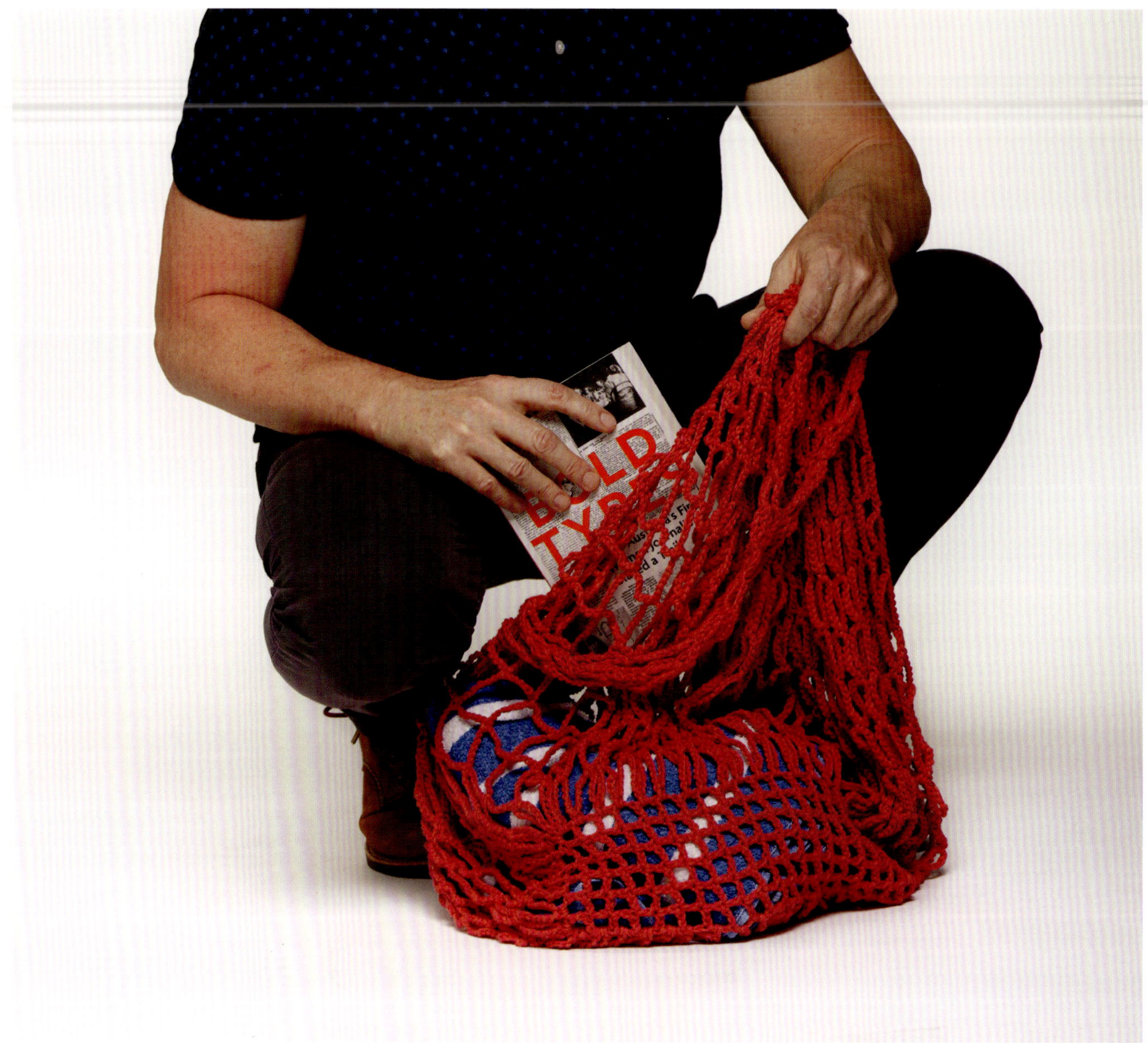

HANDLES

Work 7 ch, 1 dtr into 6th ch from hook, 2 dtr into same ch, * turn, 6 ch, 3 dtr into centre of group of dtr. Rep from * until work measures 100 cm.

Weave the band through last row of holes at the top of bag, missing 10 holes at each side. Fasten the ends securely together.

Crochet Yourself a Shopping Carry-all

RED macramé was the cord used by "Gersille" (N.S.W.) in working out as a MIRROR design this shopping carry-all.

It calls for two balls of No. 10 twine and a medium-size bone crochet hook.

Abbreviations: Ch, chain; tr, treble; sp, space; sl-st, slip-stitch; dc, double crochet; rep, repeat; d-tr, double treble.

Starting with the base of the bag, work 20 ch.

1st Row: One tr into fifth ch from hook (count as 1 sp), * 2 ch, miss 2 ch, 1 tr into next ch. Rep from * to end of row (6 sps).

2nd Row: Turn, 5 ch, 1 tr into 1 tr, * 2 ch, 1 tr into next tr. Rep from * to end of row.

Rep last row until 24 rows have been worked, completing the base.

Now work the sides around the base as follows:

Into last sp at corner 15 ch, 1 dc, 15 ch, 1 dc, 15 ch.

Into next sp 1 dc, 15 ch, 1 dc, 15 ch.

* Into next sp 1 dc, 15 ch. Rep from * to 22nd sp.

Into 23rd sp 1 dc, 15 ch, 1 dc, 15 ch.

Into corner sp 1 dc, 15 ch, 1 dc, 15 ch, 1 dc, 15 ch.

Into next sp 1 dc, 15 ch, 1 dc, 15 ch.

* Into next sp 1 dc, 15 ch. Rep from * once more.

Turn the corner in the same manner as the last corner, and rep all around the base of the bag, ending with a sl-st into the same sp as the beg of row.

2nd Row: Sl-st to centre of loop of 15 ch, * 15 ch, 1 dc into the centre of next loop. Rep from * all around, ending with sl-st to the centre of the first loop of last row.

Rep last row until nine rows of sides have been worked.

Next Row: Sl-st to centre of loop, 8 ch, 1 tr into next loop, * 5 ch, 1 tr into next loop. Rep from * all around, ending in pattern.

Next Row: Sl-st to centre of bar of 5 ch, 5 ch, 1 tr into next bar, * 2 ch, 1 tr into next bar. Rep from * all around, ending in pattern.

THE HANDLES.—Seven ch, 1 d-tr into 6th ch from hook, 2 d-tr into same ch, * turn, 6 ch, 3 d-tr into centre of group of d-tr. Rep from * until work measures 30in.

Thread through last row of holes at the top of bag, missing 10 holes at each side. Fasten the ends securely together.

"Vera": Before starting to sew, fasten a paper bag to the side of the machine with a piece of adhesive tape. Threads and scraps can be dropped into the bag while working, and there will be no picking up the bits and pieces after the job is done.

PAPER PLATES

I BEGAN experimenting with paper plates, and the results have been so fascinating and inexpensive that I pass the practice on for the benefit of my less-talented co-artists, invalids or children.

Using quick-drying enamel, my first efforts were symmetrical borders in varying colors, or simple bold designs repeated several times round the plate (using only two colors), and finished with a plain border in the contrasting shades.

Quaint motifs can easily be worked from magazine illustrations and strips. All must be varnished over in clear lacquer.

Paper doyleys, sold as low as 1½d. a dozen also offer a wealth of design which may be picked out and colored to look like mosaic, then fitted on to the paper plate and shellacked. Some doyley patterns have flowers or conventional designs which transform into really pretty pictures when the lacquer outlining is completed.

Following the design of a kindergarten Christmas card, made from shiny paper cut-outs, a simple green tree, blue house, white snow, yellow moon, all pasted on the plate, and then details, such as paths, background fir-trees and borders outlined in Indian ink, with the final outer coating of shellac, the result was well worth while.

Even the old stand-by of catalogue pictures pasted artistically and finished with waterproofing can become an attractive ornament.

Finally an attempt can be made by painting a design on the back of a glass saucer or plate, crumpling up a sheet of silver paper, and fitting the silver paper between the paper plate and the one upon which the painting is done.

If a stock-size paper plate is not available the effect can be achieved by pasting several layers of good writing paper (papier maché manner) behind the silver paper and the glass painting (giving the back a final coating of coloring lacquer).

A good mucilage glue is best, and if enamel plates are used as backgrounds it is hard to distinguish the finished work from a good china specimen.

An old-fashioned xylonite mirror had a miraculous uplift when a mosaic-patterned enamel design was gummed to the back and pastel enamelling carried out to fit the design.

Ideas are inexhaustible. Ingenuity and a little skill can produce unusual specimens at a very small cost.

S.A. ROSEMARY SUE.

For kids

Try your hand at crocheted toys and wacky wearables, as well as modern takes on traditional clothing for children.

Baby blankets and shawls are a very traditional gift for new parents and many of them are crocheted, either using motifs or with lacy stitches. We've updated the tradition with a fluoro orange pram cover (see page 118). If you want something more classic, the afghan (page 24) or the motifs we used for the hot-water bottle cover (page 32) could be worked in baby wool.

As well as the sleeveless dress (page 122) and jumper (page 130) for toddlers, there's also the bolero and pants (page 114) and the sun hat (page 140) if you're looking for clothing to crochet for children.

We've turned a couple of crochet patterns for stuffed animals into cute amigurumi-style toys that will amuse little ones for hours (see pages 126 and 144). And then there are the animal caps (page 134); these are so quick to make in 14-ply yarn that you can whip them up in plenty of time for the Easter hat parade or Book Week dress-up days at school.

Intermediate

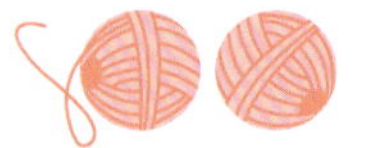

Bolero and pants

This dazzling outfit consists of tiny crocheted motifs, with matching motifs marching up the side of the pants.

The Australian Women's Weekly, 20 September 1972.

Materials: 4-ply machine-washable wool yarn, 200 g balls: 2 x main colour (MC), 1 x each of 2 contrast colours (CC1, CC2); 2.50 mm and 3.50mm crochet hooks.
Measurements: To fit 56 cm chest (actual measurement 61 cm); bolero length 25.5 cm; inside leg measurement 28 cm; outside leg measurement with waistband 47 cm. Each motif measures 5 cm square; 12 htr and 8 rows to 5 cm over main patt on pants.

MOTIF

1st round: Using CC1 and 2.50 mm hook, make 5 ch, join with sl-st to form ring, 5 ch, (1 tr in ring, 2 ch) 7 times, sl-st to 3rd of 5 ch. Break off CC1 but keep last loop on hook.
2nd round: Join CC2, sl-st in ch sp, 3 ch. (2 tr, 1 ch, 3 tr) in same sp, * 3 tr in next sp, (3 tr, 1 ch, 3 tr) in next sp, rep from * twice, 3 tr in next sp, sl-st to 3rd of 3 ch, sl-st along to 1 ch sp. Break off CC2 but keep last loop on hook.
3rd round: Join MC, sl-st in ch sp, 3 ch (2 tr, 1 ch, 3 tr) in same sp, * (3 tr in next sp) twice, (3 tr, 1 ch, 3 tr) in next 1 ch sp, rep from * twice, 3 tr in next sp twice, join with sl-st to 3rd of 3 ch. Fasten off.

BOLERO

Make 50 motifs.
Using MC, join motifs as shown in diagram on page 116.
Press only on wrong side with warm iron and damp cloth.
Join shoulder seams.

TO FINISH

1st round: With right side facing, use MC to work 1 round of dc around outside edge, working 2 dc in corners and ensuring you have a multiple of 3 sts. Join with sl-st.

The suit was made for and photographed on a three-year-old. Use a smaller or larger hook to change the size slightly. You will need to make 50 motifs for the bolero and 18 motifs for the pants.

2nd round: 1 ch, * 1 dc in each of next 3 dc, 3 ch, sl-st back into last dc to form picot, rep from * to end, working 2 dc in corners as before. Join with sl-st, fasten off.

Work the same 2 rounds around armholes.

Using double yarn, join to neck corners and work ch approximately 40 cm long on each corner. Knot ends and trim. Tie at neckline.

PANTS

Make 18 motifs and set aside.

Using 3.50 mm hook and MC make 61 ch.

Foundation row: 1 htr in 3rd ch from hook, 1 htr in each ch to end (60 htr).

Pattern row: 2 ch to turn, 1 htr in each htr to end. Rep last row until work measures 15 cm.

1st increase row: 2 ch to turn, 1 htr in each of next 27 htr, 2 htr in next htr, 1 htr in each of next 2 htr, 2 htr in next htr, 1 htr in each htr to end (62 htr). Work 2 rows without shaping.

2nd increase row: 2 ch to turn, 1 htr in each of next 28 htr, 2 htr in next htr, 1 htr in each of next 2 htr, 2 htr in next htr, 1 htr in each htr to end (64 htr).

Continue increasing in this way every 3rd row until 72 htr, then cont straight until work measures 28 cm or required length from beg.

Shape crotch: 2 ch to turn, 1 htr in each of next 31 htr, turn and work on this side only, dec 1 htr at beg next and following alternate rows. Dec 1 htr at same edge of following 4th row, then each 6th row until 26 htr remain. Cont until work measures 46 cm or required length from beg, ending at side edge. **

Work rise for back: Sl-st over 4 sts, 1 ch, 1 dc in next st, 1 htr in each htr to end, 2 ch to turn, 1 htr in each htr to last 4 htr, turn, rep last 2 rows once.

Leave 8 sts at crotch unworked, rejoin yarn to next st and complete to match 1st side to **, reversing shapings.

Fasten off.

Make 2nd leg to match 1st leg, working rise for back on 2nd side.

ARMHOLE ARMHOLE

BACK

TO COMPLETE

Neatly join front and back crotch seams. Join motifs into 2 rows of 9 motifs each and fit to straight edge at side of pants. Stitch in position, then join other straight edge to other edge of motifs. Using MC, work 5 rounds htr around waistline. Fasten off.

Fold these last 5 rounds in half to wrong side and sl-st in place to form waistband. Thread elastic through to fit. Work 2 rounds dc around lower edge of each leg. Press only on wrong side with warm iron and damp cloth.

The original pattern used Andalusian wool, which was commonly used for babywear and accessories in the 1930s. Modern 4-ply baby wool or acrylic is a good substitute. No finished dimensions are given, so the tension is not noted.

Intermediate

Pram cover

Use a contrasting colour for the backing of this coverlet to show off your intricate crochet work.

The Australian Woman's Mirror, 25 August 1936.

Materials: 4-ply acrylic yarn, 2 x 50 g balls; 3.50 mm crochet hook; 2 m narrow satin ribbon and 1 m slightly wider satin ribbon for bow; 1 m backing fabric; approximately 0.5 x 1 m batting.

Special stitches: Double treble (dtr): yoh twice, pull loop through fabric, (yoh, pull through 2 loops) twice, yoh, pull through remaining loops.

COVER

Commence with 108 ch.

1st row: Turn with 9 ch, 1 tr into 6th st, 6 ch, miss 6 sts, 12 tr into next 12 ch, 6 ch, 1 tr in 6th st, 12 tr. Rep to end of ch.

2nd row: Turn with 6 ch, 1 dc into 3rd st, 3 ch, 1 tr on single tr, 3 ch, 1 dc, 3 ch, 12 tr, 3 ch, 1 dc in 3rd st, 3 ch, 1 tr on tr, 3 ch, 1 dc in 3rd st, 12 tr. Rep to end of row.

Rep these 2 rows twice more.

7th row: Turn with 3 ch, 11 tr, 6 ch, miss 6 sts, 1 tr, 6 ch, 12 tr. Rep to end.

8th row: Turn with 3 ch, 11 tr, 3 ch, 1 dc in 3rd st, 3 ch, 1 tr, 3 ch, 1 dc in 3rd st, 12 tr. Rep to end.

Rep these 2 rows twice more.

Continue these blocks to the length required.

BORDER

1st row: Work 1 row of tr all round cover, working extra stitches into corners to keep the border flat.

2nd row: 3 ch, * 2 dtr into next 2 sts, 3 ch, miss 3. Rep from * all round.

3rd row: Work another row of tr all round.

4th row: 3 ch, 1 tr into 2nd st 3 times, 3 ch, miss 3, 1 dc, miss 3, and rep.

5th row: 3 ch, 1 tr 3 times into centre tr, 3 ch, 1 tr in top of dc, and rep.

6th row: Same as 5th row.

Weave ribbon through 2nd row of border and finish with smart bow.

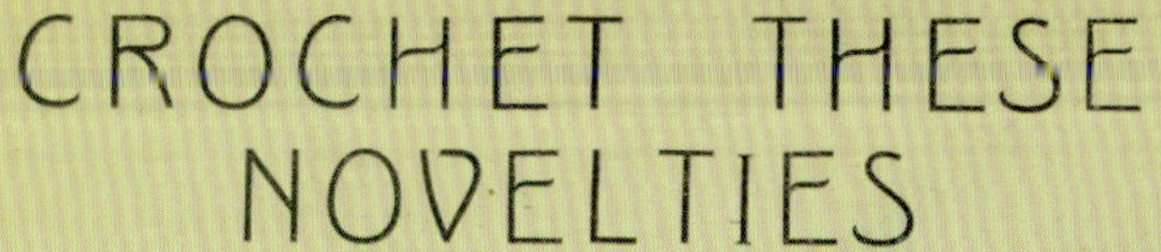

CROCHET THESE NOVELTIES

PRAM-COVER FOR BABY; MEDALLIONS FOR A LUNCHEON SET

THE crochet cover for Baby's pram (see below) requires for materials: 1 packet Andalusian wool, 1 yard pale-blue mervene for lining, 2 yards narrow ribbon and 1 yard slightly wider for bow. Use 1½ steel hook.

Abbreviations Used: Ch, chain; dc, double crochet; tr, treble; ltr, long treble; st, stitch; blk, block of treble; sp, space.

Commence with 108 ch, turn with 9 ch, 1 tr into 6th st, 6 ch, miss six sts, 12 tr into next 12 ch, 6 ch, 1 tr in 6th st, 12 tr. Repeat to end of ch.

2nd Row: Turn 6 ch, 1 dc into 3rd st, 3 ch, 1 tr on single tr, 3 ch, 1 dc, 3 ch, 12 tr, 3 ch, 1 dc in 3rd st, 3 ch, 1 tr on tr, 3 ch, 1 dc in 3rd st, 12 tr. Repeat to end of row.

Repeat these two rows twice more.

7th Row: Turn 3 ch, 11 tr, 6 ch, miss 6 sts, 1 tr, 6 ch, 12 tr. Repeat to end.

8th Row: Turn 3 ch, 11 tr, 3 ch, 1 dc in 3rd st, 3 ch, 1 tr, 3 ch, 1 dc in 3rd st, 12 tr. Repeat to end.

Repeat these two rows twice more.

Continue these blocks to the length required.

For the Border work 1 row of tr all round cover, 3 ch, * 2 ltr into next 2 sts, 3 ch, miss 3. Repeat from * all round.

Work another row of tr all round.

4th Row: 3 ch, 1 tr into 2nd st 3 times, 3 ch, miss 3, 1 dc, miss 3, and repeat.

5th Row: 3 ch, 1 tr 3 times into centre tr, 3 ch, 1 tr in top of dc, and repeat.

6th Row: Same as 5th row.

Thread ribbon through beading and finish with smart bow.

The lining coverlet should be double and an inch wider all round, and interlined with wadding. Then stitch on to the crochet cover.—ANNIE SMITH, *Mortdale, N.S.W., Designer.*

THREE mats for each person constitute the luncheon set of joined medallions in crochet pictured

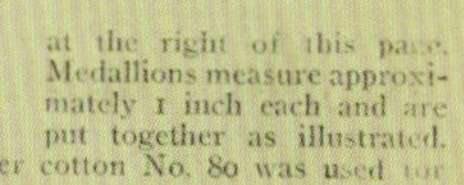

at the right of this page. Medallions measure approximately 1 inch each and are put together as illustrated.

Mercer cotton No. 80 was used for the set.

TO MAKE A MEDALLION.—8 ch, join into ring.

2nd Row: 2 ch, to form tr, 10 tr into ring, join.

3rd Row: 2 ch, over first tr of previous row, 1 ch, 1 tr, over each tr all round, join.

4th Row: Into first sp of 3rd row work 4 tr, 4 ch, 4 tr into next sp. Repeat 8 tr blks in all.

5th Row: Turn work, blk of 12 tr (4 over first ch, sp, 4 over 4 tr, 4 over next ch, sp), 8 ch. Repeat. (Four large treble blocks.)

This completes medallion.

Join second medallion after first 12 tr, 4 ch, needle under 8 ch of first medallion. Repeat.

The large mat has nine squares in first row, second row seven, and so on.

The medium mat commences with five squares, and the small one three squares.

Finish all round mats with edging of 4 chain, 1 double treble.—GERTRUDE, *Hurstville, N.S.W., Designer.*

TO MAKE UP

Use crocheted piece as a template to cut lining fabric and batting, leaving 1 cm seam allowances all around. With right sides of fabric together and batting on top, sew together around edges, leaving a small opening for turning through. Turn through and sew up the opening. Tack and then stitch the crocheted cover to the lining.

Tunisian crochet

A January 1858 issue of *Der Bazar*—the leading publisher of illustrated fancywork in Prussia of the time—described a new and 'unfamiliar type of crochet', the structure of which looked to be a mixture of crochet and knitting made using a single hooked needle. Since then, the stitch has gone through many names: crochet à la tricoter, tricot écossais, tricot Tunisien. In October of 1858, prominent English fancywork author Matilda Marian Pullan even tried to call it the 'Princess Frederick William stitch', named after Queen Victoria's eldest daughter who was married to Prince Frederick William of Prussia—before she was informed that the stitch was already referred to as the Tunisian crochet stitch.

In fact, *Der Bazar* was not even the first publication to write about Tunisian crochet. An 1857 issue of Swedish publication *Penelope* gave instructions for a child's sweater, made in *tunisisk virkstygn* (Tunisian crochet stitch), referencing instructions given on the stitch from an 1856 issue. Even before then, accounts of fabric knitted with hooked needles began as early as 1817. This, along with the stitch's myriad names, suggests that it was widely practised and had already been around for quite some time.

This specific type of crochet, now commonly referred to as either tricot or Tunisian crochet, marries together crochet and knitting, pulling distinct characteristics of the two to make beautiful fabric, which is both sturdy and light. Much like crochet, the initial foundation of Tunisian crochet is made with a chain. From there, however, like knitting, each new loop is pulled through the established row and held on the hook (forward pass) before being completed by a chain worked backwards (return pass). The forward pass for the next row is worked into the top of the previous row. Unlike knitting, the fabric is not turned and instead worked left to right and right to left. The craft produces beautiful garments with a stitch pattern like knitting, but woven together by a needle with a hooked tip using crochet techniques. (See our project on page 123.)

It wasn't long after its introduction in Europe in the late 1850s that Tunisian crochet began to appear in Australia. An 1871 column in the *Melbourne Weekly Times* includes a written pattern for a 'nice warm quilt for a bassanet' made in red and white tricot. Given the newspaper's language, and the lack of introduction to tricot as a new or unknown stitch, it is safe to conclude the stitch had been practised in Australia well before then.

Scotch fingering wool translates to a modern 3- or 4-ply, depending on the tension of your work and the size of your hook. Don't forget to make a test swatch to check, and go up or down a hook size if you need to. The technique is Tunisian crochet, using a long hook and holding all the stitches on the hook as you work across, then dropping the loops off the hook as you work back.

Search for videos on the internet if you are not familiar with this technique. The dress is worked in one piece and joined at the centre back.

Intermediate

Sleeveless dress

The oldest pattern in this book, this little dress was originally intended as a petticoat. But who wouldn't want to see those sweet stripes and pretty lacy edges?

The Colonist, 14 April 1888.

Materials: 3- or 4-ply yarn, 50 g balls: 2 x main colour (MC), 1 x contrast colour (CC); 4.50 mm Tunisian crochet hook; 4.00 mm crochet hook; 5 or 6 buttons.
Measurements: To fit a three-year-old child: chest 46 cm; length 51 cm.

PETTICOAT

With MC commence with 200 ch for the bottom of the dress. Pick up each stitch of the chain as in ordinary Tunisian crochet, and draw back in the usual manner. Work another 2 rows with MC. Then 2 rows with CC and 2 rows with MC.
7th row: CC.
8th row: Using CC, pick up 20 sts with the 1st st already on the needle (21 sts), pick up 2 tog, 21 sts, 2 tog, 12 sts, 2 tog, 21 sts, 2 tog, 34 sts, 2 tog, 21 sts, 2 tog, 12 sts, 2 tog, 21 sts, 2 tog, 21 sts, and draw back as usual (192 sts).
Work 2 rows with MC, then 2 rows with CC.
13th row: MC.
14th row: Using MC, pick up 19 sts, 2 tog, 20 sts, 2 tog, 12 sts, 2 tog, 20 sts, 2 tog, 32 sts, 2 tog, 20 sts, 2 tog, 12 sts, 2 tog, 20 sts, 2 tog, 20 sts and draw back (184 sts).
Work 2 rows with CC.
17th row: MC.
18th row: Using MC, pick up 18 sts, 2 tog, 19 sts, 2 tog, 12 sts, 2 tog, 19 sts, 2 tog, 30 sts, 2 tog, 19 sts, 2 tog, 12 sts, 2 tog, 19 sts, 2 tog, 19 sts, and draw back (176 sts).
Work 2 rows with CC.
21st row: MC.
22nd row: Using MC, pick up 17 sts, 2 tog, 18 sts, 2 tog, 12 sts, 2 tog, 18 sts, 2 tog, 28 sts,

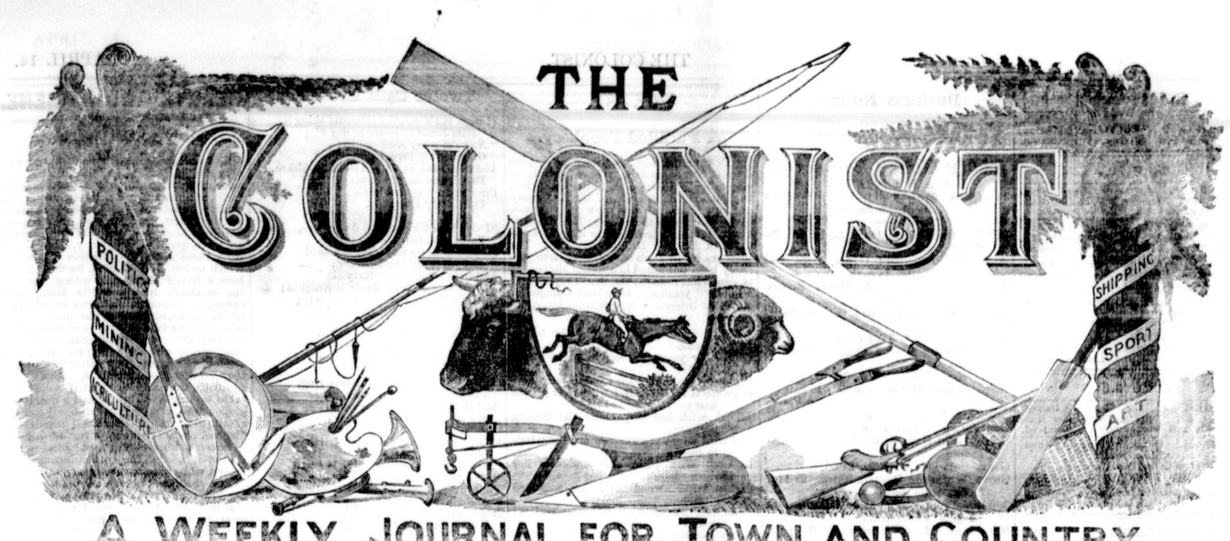
THE COLONIST
A WEEKLY JOURNAL FOR TOWN AND COUNTRY.
VOL. I. NO. XIII. LAUNCESTON, SATURDAY, APRIL 14, 1888. PRICE: FOURPENCE.

2 tog, 18 sts, 2 tog, 12 sts, 2 tog, 18 sts, 2 tog, 18 sts, and draw back (168 sts).

Work 2 rows with CC.

The remainder of the dress is worked in MC.

26th row: 16 sts, 2 tog, 17 sts, 2 tog, 12 sts, 2 tog, 17 sts, 2 tog, 26 sts, 2 tog, 17 sts, 2 tog, 12 sts, 2 tog, 17 sts, 2 tog, 17 sts, and draw back (160 sts). Work 8 ch at the end (these 8 sts are worked in plain Tunisian crochet in following rows and are not counted in the decrease instructions below.)

30th row: 15 sts, 2 tog, 16 sts, 2 tog, 12 sts, 2 tog, 16 sts, 2 tog, 24 sts, 2 tog, 16 sts, 2 tog, 12 sts, 2 tog, 16 sts, 2 tog, 16 sts, and draw back (152 sts).

34th row: 14 sts, 2 tog, 15 sts, 2 tog, 12 sts, 2 tog, 15 sts, 2 tog, 22 sts, 2 tog, 15 sts, 2 tog, 12 sts, 2 tog, 15 sts, 2 tog, 15 sts, and draw back (144 sts).

38th row: 13 sts, 2 tog, 14 sts, 2 tog, 12 sts, 2 tog, 14 sts, 2 tog, 18 sts, 2 tog, 14 sts, 2 tog, 12 sts, 2 tog, 14 sts, 2 tog, 14 sts, and draw back (136 sts).

42nd row: 12 sts, 2 tog, 13 sts, 2 tog, 12 sts, 2 tog, 13 sts, 2 tog, 16 sts, 2 tog, 13 sts, 2 tog, 12 sts, 2 tog, 13 sts, 2 tog, 13 sts, and draw back (128 sts).

48th row: 12 sts, 2 tog, 12 sts, 2 tog, 12 sts, 2 tog, 12 sts, 2 tog, 16 sts, 2 tog, 12 sts, 2 tog, 12 sts, 2 tog, 12 sts, 2 tog, 12 sts, and draw back (120 sts).

Work 30 rows on the 120 sts, including the 8 for the 'lap'. This brings you to the armhole.

For the 1st half of the back, pick up 32 sts, work 16 rows and fasten off. Pick up the last 12 sts and work 8 rows thereon for a shoulder strap. Fasten off.

Miss 6 sts from where you divided for the armhole, pick up 50 sts for the front, and work 16 rows. Then, for the shoulder strap, pick up 11 sts (1 already on the needle making 12), work 8 rows. Fasten off.

Pick up the last 12 sts for another shoulder strap, work 8 rows. Fasten off.

Miss 6 sts from the division for the armhole, pick sts to the end (25 sts) and work 16 rows. For the shoulder strap, pick up 11 sts and work 8 rows. Fasten off.

Sew up the shoulder seams and join the back of the skirt as far as the additional 8 sts for the 'lap'. Sew these under the right side.

Using the crochet hook, work a row of single crochet round the neck and shoulders, down the right-hand side of the placket hole and around the armholes.

Round the neck, armholes and bottom of skirt work an edge: 1 dc into a st of the single crochet, * 2 ch; 2 tr on the dc, miss a st of the single, 1 dc on the next and repeat from *.

Sew 5 or 6 buttons on the 'lap' down the back of the bodice, and on the opposite edge work buttonholes with a wool needle.

Originally designed as an old-fashioned baby bottle cover, we reworked the pattern to turn it into a toy.

Intermediate

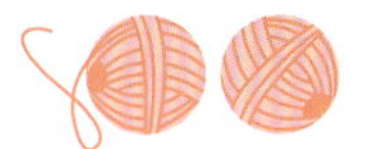

Teddy bear

This cute bear is made in amigurumi style, ideal for cuddles from children of all ages!

The Australian Women's Weekly, 20 September 1978.

Materials: Large teddy: 8-ply cotton yarn, 2 x 50 g balls; 3.00 mm crochet hook. Small teddy: 4-ply cotton yarn, 50 g balls: 1 x main colour and 1 x contrast colour (if using two colours); 2.00 mm crochet hook. Both: 8 mm safety eyes; polyfil stuffing; black embroidery thread; stitch markers.

Measurements: Large teddy: 15 cm tall in sitting position. Small teddy: 13 cm tall.

Tension: 11 dc and 14 rows to 5 cm on 3.00 mm hook.

Special stitches: Decrease 1 double crochet (dec 1 dc): (insert hook in next st, yoh and draw through a loop) twice, yoh and draw through 3 loops on hook.

HEAD

Crochet in the round for all body parts, placing a stitch marker at beg of each round.

Begin with a magic ring (tutorials are available on the internet for this).

1st round: 6 dc in magic ring. Pull ends of yarn to tighten ring.

2nd round: 2 dc in each dc (12 sts).

3rd round: (1 dc, 2 dc in next dc) rep to end (18 sts).

4th round: (2 dc, 2 dc in next dc) rep to end (24 sts).

5th round: (3 dc, 2 dc in next dc) rep to end (30 sts).

6th round: (4 dc, 2 dc in next dc) rep to end (36 sts).

7th round: (5 dc, 2 dc in next dc) rep to end (42 sts).

8th round: (6 dc, 2 dc in next dc) rep to end (48 sts).

9th to 16th rounds: 1 dc in each dc. Insert safety eyes between rows 10 and 11, approximately 7 stitches apart.

17th round: (6 dc, dec 1 dc) rep to end (42 sts).

18th round: (5 dc, dec 1 dc) rep to end (36 sts).

19th round: (4 dc, dec 1 dc) rep to end (30 sts).

Begin stuffing, making it fairly firm.

20th round: (3 dc, dec 1 dc) rep to end (24 sts).
21st round: (2 dc, dec 1 dc) rep to end (18 sts).
22nd round: (1 dc, dec 1 dc) rep to end (22 sts).
Fasten off, leaving a long tail.
Finish stuffing.
Take a needle and pull the tail through the front loops of remaining 12 sts and pull until the hole closes.

MUZZLE

Begin with a magic ring.
1st round: 6 dc in magic ring. Pull ends of yarn to tighten ring.
2nd round: 2 dc in each dc (12 sts).
3rd round: (2 dc, 2 dc in next dc) rep to end (16 sts).
4th round: (3 dc, 2 dc in next dc) rep to end (20 sts).
5th round: (4 dc, 2 dc in next dc) rep to end (24 sts).
6th round: (5 dc, 2 dc in next dc) rep to end (28 sts).
7th round: (6 dc, 2 dc in next dc) rep to end (32 sts).
8th round: (7 dc, 2 dc in next dc) rep to end (36 sts).
Fasten off, leaving long tail for sewing to head.

BODY

Working from bottom up, begin with a magic ring.
1st round: 6 dc in magic ring. Pull ends of yarn to tighten ring.
2nd round: 2 dc in each dc (12 sts).
3rd round: (1 dc, 2 dc in next dc) rep to end (18 sts).
4th round: (2 dc, 2 dc in next dc) rep to end (24 sts).
5th round: (3 dc, 2 dc in next dc) rep to end (30 sts).
6th round: (4 dc, 2 dc in next dc) rep to end (36 sts).
7th round: (5 dc, 2 dc in next dc) rep to end (42 sts).
8th to 19th rounds: 1 dc in each dc.
20th round: (5 dc, dec 1 dc) rep to end (36 sts).
21st round: (4 dc, dec 1 dc) rep to end (30 sts).
Begin stuffing, making it fairly firm.
22nd round: (3 dc, dec 1 dc) rep to end (24 sts).
23rd round: (2 dc, dec 1 dc) rep to end (18 sts).
24th round: (1 dc, dec 1 dc) rep to end (22 sts).
Fasten off, leaving a long tail. Finish stuffing.

LEGS

Begin with a magic ring.
1st round: 6 dc in magic ring. Pull ends of yarn to tighten ring.
2nd round: 2 dc in each dc (12 sts).
3rd round: (1 dc, 2 dc in next dc) rep to end (18 sts).
4th to 6th rounds: 1 dc in each dc.
7th round: (1 dc, dec 1 dc) rep to end (12 sts).
8th to 11th rounds: 1 dc in each dc.
12th round: (2 dc, dec 1 dc) rep to end (9 sts).
13th to 15th round: 1 dc in each dc.
Lightly stuff leg about ¾ full: teddy will sit better if limbs are not overfilled.
Pinch the top of leg together and sl-st closed.
Fasten off.
Make two.

ARMS

Begin with a magic ring.

1st round: 6 dc in magic ring. Pull ends of yarn to tighten ring.

2nd round: (1 dc, 2 dc in next dc) rep to end (9 sts).

3rd round: (2 dc in next dc, 1 dc) rep to end (14 sts).

4th to 17th rounds: 1 dc in each dc. Lightly stuff arm about ¾ full.

Pinch the top of arm together and sl-st closed. Fasten off.

Make two.

EARS

Begin with a magic ring.

1st round: 6 dc in magic ring. Pull ends of yarn to tighten ring.

2nd round: 2 dc in each dc (12 sts).

3rd round: (1 dc, 2 dc in next dc) rep to end (18 sts).

4th round: 1 dc in each dc. Fasten off, leaving long tail for attaching to head.

Make two.

TAIL

Begin with a magic ring.

1st round: 6 dc in magic ring. Pull ends of yarn to tighten ring.

2nd round: 2 dc in each dc (12 sts).

3rd round: (1 dc, 2 dc in next dc) rep to end (18 sts).

4th round: 1 dc in each dc.

5th round: (dec 1 dc, 1 dc) rep to end (12 sts). Fasten off, leaving long tail for attaching to body.

TO MAKE UP

Sew muzzle to head, positioning 1 row below the eyes. Stuff as you sew to make it firm.

Attach head to body.

Attach legs to the lower body, facing outwards at an angle. Between rows 2 and 5 towards the back of the body is a good position.

Attach the tail at centre back, at round 5 or 6.

Attach the arms, at round 21.

Attach the ears between rounds 8 and 9 of the head, sewing on a slight curve.

Embroider the nose and mouth.

Made in 4-ply baby wool, this is designed for a one- to two-year-old. To make a bigger size, you could simply increase the number of stitches across and the number of stripes in length until you get the desired size. Don't forget to adjust the starting point for the sleeves if you do this.

Beginner

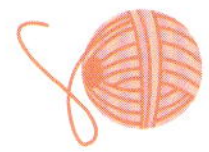

Short-sleeved jumper

This little jumper may be made with long or short sleeves. The waistband and yoke are knitted in rib.

The Australian Woman's Mirror, 21 March 1944.

Materials: 4-ply baby wool, 50 g balls: 2 (3 for long sleeves) x main colour (MC) and 1 x contrast colour (CC); 2.5 mm crochet hook; 2.75 mm knitting needles; 4 x 15 mm buttons.
Measurements: To fit 51 cm chest; length 30 cm.
Tension: 12 tr and 8 rows to 5 cm.

BACK

Starting with the 1st crochet row of the back, the jumper is worked in one piece with the knitted yoke in the middle, and the front is worked from top to bottom.
With MC and crochet hook, make 71 ch, turn, 1 tr into 3rd ch, 1 tr into each ch to end of row (69 sts).
Turn with 2 ch, work 2 rows of 1 tr into each tr, turning with 1 ch on 3rd row.
4th row: Break off MC and join on CC. Work 1 dc into each tr.
Break off CC and join MC. Rep 3 tr rows and 1 dc row to 34th row. Work 2 more rows, dec 1 st at each end, and end on dc row.

TO MAKE YOKE

Use the crochet hook to draw a loop through each dc and slip on to knitting needle (65 sts).
Work 14 rows of K1, P1 rib.
15th row: Rib 10 sts, cast off 45 sts, rib 10 sts.
16th row (front neckline): Rib 10 sts, cast on 45 sts, rib 10 sts (65 sts).
Work 14 more rows of rib.

FRONT

Break off MC and join CC. 1 dc into each knitted st to end of row and continue front in 3 rows tr in MC, 1 row dc in CC patt for 32 rows.
Use the crochet hook to draw a loop through each dc and slip on to knitting needle as for yoke.
Rib 15 rows as for yoke. Cast off.
Knit up 69 sts along waist edge of back and rib 15 rows to match front. Cast off.

CROCHET JUMPER FOR TODDLER

DESIGNED for the MIRROR by "Amur," this crochet jumper

Fourteen more rows of rib.

dc into each
other end of
Press well, s
and under slee

Junk, B

WHEN orga
fair aske
tions Mrs. Ne
her opportu
rid of some
termed the
in her home
pied by he
law, now de
Down fro
shelves can
crockery to
on the lower
the bride's o
ware.
The morning
the back seat
calling for gif
high with her
Later, arrivin
herself, she
twinge of cons
haps it was no
ing to have p
that rubbish o
suspecting pron
Odds and Ends
Impulsively
the secretary
subscription a
distance from
stall. But late
approaching
charge of Odd
Mrs. N.W.
misgivings an
creep away.
Her unease
astonishment.
"Thank you
your handsome gifts!" greet
was most generous of you. T
hot cakes. Lady —— paid te

SLEEVES

Start at left front 4th dc stripe from neckline. 2 tr over each end tr of rows, 1 tr into each end dc, 1 tr into each end st of knitted rows. Cont across shoulder to same stripe on back. Turn with 2 ch.

For short sleeves: Cont work in patt as for back to 16th row, dec 1 st at each end of 2nd tr row in each MC stripe. Finish off with 3 rows of dc in CC.

For long sleeves: Cont work in patt as for back to 24th row, dec 1 st at each end of 2nd tr row in each MC stripe. Work 12 more rows without dec. Knit up sts with knitting needle, rib 16 rows to match waistline. Cast off.

TO MAKE UP

Make two button loops at each end of front neckline. Join on MC at front end st of neck and use crochet hook: 4 ch, 1 dc into 5th knitted st, 4 ch, miss 4 sts, 1 dc into next st, turn, 6 dc into each loop. Rep at other side of neck.

Press well, then sew up side and sleeve seams using a flat seam.

Finger crochet

From the first known mention of crochet in sixteenth-century Scotland to present-day Australia, crochet has shifted through many names, techniques and tools, from shepherd's knitting to filet crochet and flat bone hooks to the modern-day steel hook. But the basics of crochet can be replicated using just your fingers and some yarn.

As early as the eighteenth century, women were documented practising crochet on their fingers. In a comprehensive study on embroidery in 1770, Charles Germain de Saint-Aubin noted that tambour embroidery (an earlier predecessor of contemporary crochet) could be done both on the fingers and with a hooked needle. Even earlier, in a 1653 patent granted for passementiers—a type of chain-stitch embroidery or 'chains in the air'—the textile is also described as being done with a 'needle, thimbles, on a crochet or on the fingers'.

Finger crochet has now become a common technique in its own right and is often used as an introductory tool to the craft for young ones and people newly picking up the hobby or as a way to make up bulky garments, blankets and other items quickly and cheaply. Due to the way crochet is made, with the foundation of every piece being a chain and the loops interlocking both laterally and vertically, the stitches learned on the fingers can be completely transferred onto a hook, and vice versa.

This is unique to crochet, and one of the many reasons why finger crocheting is such a valuable, fun skill to practice. It can also develop hand-eye coordination and fine motor dexterity. To top it all off, finger crochet is portable, quick, affordable and simple.

These are quick projects designed in 14-ply yarn. If you can't find the colours you want in 14-ply, you can use 2 strands of 8-ply together.

This also allows you to introduce some variegation, by using two shades of the same colour (for example, for the cat) or two different colours (for example, the lion) to get a range of effects.

Intermediate

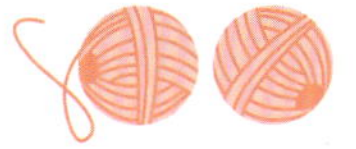

Animal caps

Keep small heads and ears warm the fun way with these zany caps, all made with variations on one basic pattern.

The Australian Women's Weekly, 5 April 1978.

Materials: Chunky 14-ply yarn, 40 g balls; 5.00 and 5.50 mm crochet hooks.
Lion: 3 x main colour (MC), 1 x each of 2 contrast colours (CC1, CC2), small quantities of 3 x bright colours (BC1, BC2, BC3).
Cat: 3 x main colour (MC), 1 x contrast colour (CC1), small quantities of 3 x bright colours (BC1, BC2, BC3); 3.00 mm crochet hook.
Rabbit: 3 x main colour (MC), 1 x contrast colour (CC); pipe-cleaners or plastic-covered bendable wire.
Bee: 1 x main colour (MC), 1 x 1st contrast colour (CC1), 2 x 2nd contrast colour (CC3), small quantity of bright colour (BC); stiff non-woven interfacing.
Measurements: Basic cap fits children three to eight years old.
Special stitches: Increase 1 double crochet (inc 1 dc): 2 dc in same place; Increase 1 treble (inc 1 tr): 2 tr in same place; Decrease 1 double crochet (dec 1 dc): (insert hook in next st, yoh and draw through a loop) twice, yoh and draw through all loops on hook; Decrease 1 treble (dec 1 tr): leaving last loop of each tr on hook, work 1 tr in each of next 2 sts, yoh and draw through all loops on hook.

BASIC CAP

With 5.50 mm hook, make 4 ch, sl-st to 1st ch to form circle.
1st round: 3 ch, 11 tr in circle, sl-st to top of 3 ch (12 tr).
2nd round: (3 ch 1 tr) in 1st tr, 2 tr in each tr to end, sl-st to top of 3 ch.
Cont in rounds of tr, evenly inc 8 tr on next and every round until 56 tr. Work 1 round of tr without increasing.
Next round: Start shaping for face. 3 ch, 1 tr in each tr to last 17 tr, turn. Cont on these 39 tr, working to and fro, for further 4 rows, then at end of 4th row, make 17 ch for under chin and join to top of 3 ch with sl-st.
Next round: 3 ch, 1 tr in tr and in each ch to end, sl-st to top of 3 ch (56 tr).
Cont in rounds of tr, evenly dec 8 tr on next round, then work 2 rounds more without decreasing. Fasten off.

LION

With MC only, make basic cap.

Ears (make 2): With 5.00 mm hook and CC1, make 4 ch, sl-st to 1st ch to form circle, 1 ch, work 8 dc in circle, sl-st to 1st dc.

Cont in rounds of dc, evenly inc 8 dc on every round until 24 dc. Fasten off.

Flowers: With 5.00 mm hook and coloured yarn, make 4 ch, sl-st to 1st ch to form circle. (4ch, 1 dc) 5 times in circle, fasten off but leave long tails for tying. Make as many as you like.

To finish: Securely attach ears in positions. Cut CC1, CC2 and remaining MC to lengths of 20 cm (see note), then fold a length in half and pass the folded end around a tr, then pull the ends through the fold and pull firmly, to make the mane. Rep as many times as you like. Tie a flower to a strand of mane as desired.

Note: The easiest way is to cut a piece of thick cardboard 10 cm wide. Wrap the yarn around it and cut the yarn along one edge of the card-board to create 20 cm lengths.

CAT

With MC only, make basic cap until end of the dec round is reached at neck, then with CC work 2 rounds of dc, then with MC work 1 round of tr. Fasten off.

Outer ears: With 5.00 mm hook and MC, make 10 ch, then work 4 rows of dc, then dec 1 dc each end of next and every following 2nd row until 1 dc remaining, then work 1 round of dc around all edges, sl-st to 1st dc, fasten off. Make two.

Inner ears: With 5.00 mm hook and CC, make 8 ch. Work 1 row of dc, then dec 1 dc each end of next and every following 2nd row until

1 dc remaining. Fasten off. Make two.

Whiskers: With 3.00 mm hook and CC, make 13 ch, work sl-st in each ch to end, fasten off. Make six.

To finish: Match up ears and sew on to positions. Securely attach whiskers. With 3.00 mm hook and BC1, make 18 ch. Fasten off, then attach to centre front neck for buckle. With wool needle, BC2 and BC3, embroider alternating colour French knots on collar.

RABBIT

With MC only, make basic cap.

Inner ears: With 5.00 mm hook and CC, make 6 ch. * Work in dc. Inc 1 dc at centre of 4th row, then on following 6th row once, then dec 1 dc at centre of following 6th row. * Work 3 rows without dec. Dec 1 dc each end of next row. Make two.

Next Row: ** 1 ch, (dec 1 dc) twice.

Next Row: 1 ch, dec 1 dc, fasten off.

Outer ears: With 5.00 mm hook and MC, make 8 ch. Work from * to * of inner ear once. Work 5 rows without dec. Dec 1 dc each end of next and following 2nd row once, then finish as inner ear from **, then work 1 row of dc on long edges, fasten off. Make two.

To finish: Match up pair of inner and outer ears and insert pipe-cleaners or wire to provide stiffness. Sew into positions, catching pipe-cleaners to cap. With right side facing and 5.00 mm hook, join MC at centre of chin, (3 ch, sl-st to 1st of 3 ch, 1 dc in st 5 mm away from prev st) rep round all edges of face opening, sl-st to 1st dc. Fasten off.

BEE

Make basic cap working in stripes of 1 round MC, 2 rounds CC1 and 2 rounds MC. Rep last 4 rounds, but ending with 1 round of MC.

Large wings: With 5.00 mm hook and CC2, make 7 ch. Work in dc. Inc 1 dc each end of 2nd row, then following 4th row once (10 dc). Work further 13 rows without inc. Dec 1 dc at beg of every row until 4 dc remain, fasten off. Join CC2 at lower edge, evenly work in dc around outer edges, fasten off.
Make two.

Small wings: Work as large wing but working 8 rows after last inc instead of 13 rows, then finish as large wing. Make two.

Base of antennae: With 5.00 mm hook and BC, work as for flower of Lion Cap. Make two.

Antennae: With 5.00 mm hook, and CC1, make ch until 18 cm long, 1 dc in 2nd ch from hook, 1 dc in each ch to end, turn. 1 ch, work sl-st in each of foundation ch at base of each dc to end, fasten off. Curl one end and catch to keep curl in place. Place other end of antenna to centre of base of antenna, then securely sew in position. Work other antenna in same way.

To finish: Cut out interfacing material 5 mm smaller than each wing segment, then neatly sew on to back of each wing. Match up large and small wings, then securely sew on at back of cap.

mad caps to crochet for kids
Womens Weekly

Beginner

Sun hat

Cute beach hat to top off shiny curls is crocheted in easy shell pattern.

The Australian Women's Weekly, 24 January 1973

Materials: 8-ply bamboo-cotton blend yarn, 3 x 50 g balls; 4.50 mm crochet hook.
Measurements: To fit a child 5–8 years old.

HAT

Make 6 ch, join with sl-st to form ring.
1st round: 3 ch, 11 tr in ring, sl-st into 3rd ch.
2nd round: 3 ch, 3 tr in 1st tr, * miss 1 tr, 1 ch, 4 tr in next tr, rep from * to end, 1 ch, join with sl-st to 3rd ch (six 4 tr shells) sl-st to centre sp of 1st shell.
3rd round: 3 ch, 3 tr in same sp, * 1 ch, 4 tr in next 1 ch sp, 1 ch, 4 tr in centre sp of 4 tr shell, rep from * ending with 1 ch, 4 tr in last 1 ch sp, 1 ch, join with sl-st to 3rd ch, sl-st to centre sp of 4 tr shell.
4th round: 3 ch, 3 tr in same sp, 2 ch, * 4 tr in centre sp of next 4 tr shell, 2 ch, rep from * to end, sl-st in 3rd ch, sl-st to centre sp of 4 tr shell.
5th round: 3 ch, 3 tr in same sp, 3 ch, * 4 tr in centre of shell, 3 ch, rep from * to end, sl-st to 3rd ch, sl-st to centre of 4 tr shell.
6th round: 3 ch, 5 tr in same sp, 3 ch, * 6 tr in centre of shell, 3 ch, rep from * to end, sl-st in 3rd ch, sl-st to centre of 6 tr shell.
7th round: 3 ch, 5 tr in same sp, 2 ch, * 6 tr in centre of 6 tr shell, 2 ch, rep from * to end, sl-st in 3rd ch, sl-st to centre of 6 tr shell.
8th round: 3 ch, 5 tr in same sp, 1 ch, * 6 tr in centre of 6 tr shell, 1 ch, rep from * to end, sl-st in 3rd ch, sl-st to centre of 6 tr shell.
9th and 10th rounds: Rep 8th round.
11th round: 3 ch, 5 tr in same sp, 1 ch, * 6 tr in centre of 6 tr shell, 1 ch, rep from * to end, sl-st in 3rd ch.
12th round: 1 dc in each tr and 2 dc in 1 ch sp all round, ending with 1 dc in 3rd ch (94 dc).
13th round: 1 dc in each dc.
14th round: * 1 dc in next 4 dc, 2 dc in next dc, rep from * to end. Work 9 more rounds in dc. Fasten off.

Crocheted in 8-ply yarn, this hat is designed for a five to eight-year-old child but could also be made for an adult by adding one shell pattern around and one extra round of shells, as well as a few extra rounds of dc for a bigger brim.

A stitch marker to mark the beginning of the rounds is useful. Note that cotton yarn will have a softer drape than wool yarn.

Continuing –

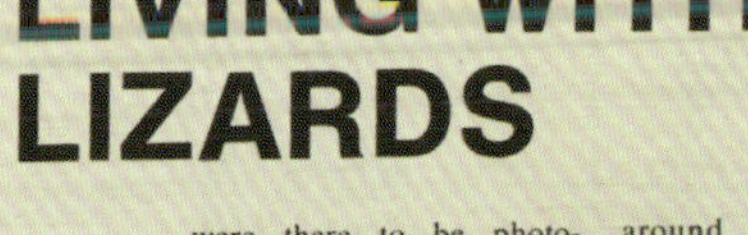

LIVING WITH LIZARDS

From page 23

Notable were the huge eyes in his rather bulgy head. The upward bow of his mouth gave him an always grinning expression. His legs were awkwardly thin and long, but it was his tail that was most striking: it was carrot-shaped but ended in a little round knob.

Harry proved to be a real lizard-character, too, though he never became as friendly as Fatso. He wanted to be left alone and mind his own business, which consisted mainly of digging burrows all over the floor of his cage.

Being nocturnal like all Australian geckos (there are 60-odd kinds), he slept all day hidden in his favorite hole and would only appear soon after sunset to begin his work. When fed with grasshoppers, crickets, and cockroaches, however, Harry could get very excited. He liked crickets most.

When he saw one in his cage he would stalk it the way a cat stalks a mouse. Very slowly he would move closer, only his tail twitching nervously; then he would suddenly leap forward and grab the cricket with his strong jaws, and eat it with relish.

It soon became known to our friends that we had some kind of a house-zoo, and remarks like "What's Fatso doing?" or "How is Harry?" featured in many a conversation.

While Fatso, Harry, and those two mulga goannas became permanent residents in our flat, many other lizards, tortoises, and frogs too paid short visits to be photographed.

We had lived in Sydney for a year when we both felt the urge to go somewhere else again. We bought a caravan to hook on to our old and battered but very reliable Land Rover and set out for Western Australia.

Gunther had never been in that State, and quite a number of goanna species were there to be photographed by him.

Our pets, of course, came with us.

The first stop was at Renmark, S.A., where we visited friend Joe Bredl's reptile park and Gunther obtained photographs of Australia's largest goanna, the prettily colored perenty.

On the Eyre Peninsula a frightful looking but harmless thorny or mountain devil crossed our path to be photographed. On the Nullarbor it was a blue-tongue lizard; at Wave Rock some dragons; and so we went on.

Given their own room

In Western Australia, Gunther had a job to go to at Port Hedland, and on arrival there we prepared for a long stay. An annexe was attached to the van, giving more privacy and twice as much room.

Fatso, Harry, and Company, who had travelled in special containers and who looked as well as ever, moved back into their cages set up inside the annexe. For nothing in the world was I going to have them inside the van. The goannas had grown almost to their full size by now, Fatso being nearly twice as big as the others.

Soon after our arrival, our friend Steve Swanson, who had given us all the lizards, arrived to work in Port Hedland, and he and Gunther came together as a team, as they had done before. Steve had a permit to collect reptiles for museums, as in Western Australia all animals of this kind, with the exception of venomous snakes, are protected by law.

However, I did not plan to spend all my spare time chasing lizards and snakes, so Gunther and I came to a compromise. One weekend he would take me to a beach, and the next weekend I would join him and Steve on their photographic runs around the semi-desert district.

Sometimes we would go on night drives along the 21 miles of bitumen road toward Broome, as many reptiles – particularly frogs – could be found only at these hours, and could easily be seen on the bitumen.

Everything collected was photographed, then released.

Fatso, Harry, and Company did very well, and soon were favorites with our new friends at Hedland. However, time was running out for Harry. He had come to us as an adult and age began to tell. One day he quietly died.

Summer came and with it the heat. Even lizards used to the climate began to suffer, and we decided to send Fatso and the mulga goannas to a friend down south who was also keen on reptiles. We still kept lizards though, even if only for a day or so till they had been put on film.

The months raced by, and before we knew it the time had come for us to return to the eastern States.

The stay in the west had been very successful, and today Gunther has to put only three more species of goannas on film to have a full record of all the Australian species.

We are now working at Gladstone, Queensland. My husband is still studying goannas, and we also have a couple of new ones as pets.

Our annexe, however, is crowded with fishtanks, because Gunther is now concentrating mainly on freshwater fish.

He feels that something has to be done to protect this kind of Australian wildlife. More and more rivers and creeks are becoming polluted, and many other factors play a role in the decline of freshwater fauna without people being aware of it.

In all kinds of conservation the education of people through articles, books, and talks, and the exhibition of live specimens in zoos and nature parks, is very important. (It would be hard to convince people of the need for conservation if no one knew what to conserve.)

Well, while I am sitting behind the typewriter for a change, Gunther sits in front of his photo-fishtank in the annexe, trying to photograph a very **common** little spangled perch – which, by the sound of things, simply won't pose . . .

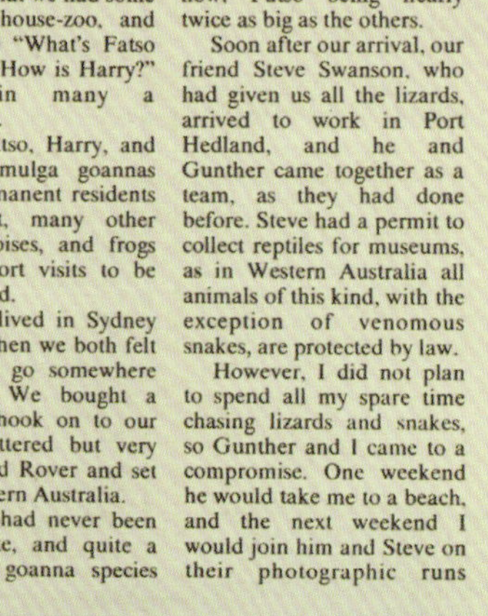

Close up of the spiny ...

Quick to crochet

HOLIDAY TOGS

The original pattern included instructions for knitting a red hooded cape for a doll and a grandma outfit too. You can find the pattern for the other pieces on Trove. We've made him up in two sizes.

Intermediate

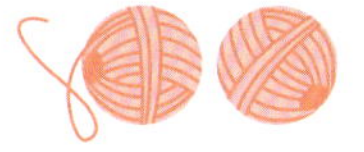

Big bad wolf

The Big Bad Wolf (wearing his knitted pants) was waiting in the woods. 'Hi, Little Red Riding Hood,' he whistled, 'you look just great.'

The Australian Women's Weekly, 17 May 1972

Materials:
Small wolf: 4-ply cotton yarn, 50 g balls: 2 x body colour (BC), 1 x overalls colour (OC); 2.00 mm crochet hook; 2.25 mm knitting needles. Large wolf: 5-ply cotton yarn, 50 g balls: 2 x body colour (BC), 1 x overalls colour (OC); 3.50 mm crochet hook; 3.75 mm knitting needles. Both: 8 mm safety eyes; black embroidery thread; 2 buttons; 1 pipe-cleaner for tail; polyfil stuffing; stitch markers.
Measurements: Small wolf: 24 cm tall. Large wolf: 30 cm tall.
Special stitches: Decrease 1 double crochet (dec 1 dc): (insert hook in next st, yoh and draw through a loop) twice, yoh and draw through 3 loops on hook; Loop: insert hook in next st, place 2 fingers of opposite hand under hook, wind yarn 2 times around hook and fingers, then around hook once, draw all 4 loops through st, yoh and draw through all 5 loops on hook, 1 ch.

HEAD

Crochet in the round for all body parts, placing a stitch marker at beg of each round.
Begin with a magic ring (tutorials are available on the internet if you don't know how to do this).
1st round: 6 dc in magic ring. Pull ends of yarn to tighten ring.
2nd round: 2 dc in each dc (12 sts).
3rd round: (1 dc, 2 dc in next dc) rep to end (18 sts).
4th to 7th rounds: 1 dc in each dc.
8th round: Start to shape forehead. (1 dc, 2 dc in next dc) rep 4 times, 10 dc (22 sts).
9th to 12th rounds: 1 dc in each dc.
13th round: 3 dc, (2 dc in next dc, 2 dc) rep 3 times, 1 dc in each dc to end (25 sts).
14th round: 1 dc in each dc.
15th round: 3 dc, (2 dc in next dc, 3 dc) rep 3 times, 1 dc in each dc to end (28 sts).
16th round: 1 dc in each dc.

17th round: 3 dc, (2 dc in next dc, 4 dc) rep 3 times, 1 dc in each dc to end (31 sts).
18th round: 1 dc in each dc.
19th round: 3 dc, (2 dc in next dc, 5 dc) rep 3 times, 1 dc in each dc to end (34 sts).
20th round: 1 dc in each dc.
21st round: 3 dc, (2 dc in next dc, 6 dc) rep 3 times, 1 dc in each dc to end (37 sts).
Insert safety eyes between rounds 17 and 18, 5 sts from start of round and 7 sts apart.
22nd to 24th rounds: 1 dc in each dc.
25th round: (7 dc, dec 1 dc) rep 4 times, 1 dc (33 sts).
26th round: (6 dc, dec 1 dc) rep 4 times, 1 dc (29 sts).
27th round: (5 dc, dec 1 dc) rep 4 times, 1 dc (25 sts).
28th round: (4 dc, dec 1 dc) rep 4 times, 1 dc (21 sts).
Begin stuffing, making it fairly firm.
29th round: (3 dc, dec 1 dc) rep 4 times, 1 dc (18 sts).
30th round: (1 dc, dec 1 dc) rep to end (12 sts).
31st round: (dec 1 dc) rep to end (6 sts).
Fasten off, leaving a long tail.
Finish stuffing.

LEGS AND BODY

(Make two legs, then join together and cont with body.)
1st leg: * Begin with a magic ring.
1st round: 6 dc in magic ring. Pull ends of yarn to tighten ring.
2nd round: 2 dc in each dc (12 sts).
3rd round: (3 dc, 2 dc in next dc) rep 3 times (15 sts).
4th to 7th rounds: 1 dc in each dc.
8th round: (3 dc, dec 1 dc) rep 3 times (12 sts).
9th to 23rd rounds: 1 dc in each dc. *
Fasten off. Stuff leg firmly with polyfil.
2nd leg: Work as 1st leg from * to * but do not fasten off. Stuff firmly with polyfil.
24th round: Begin new round on 2nd leg, 12 dc, 4 ch, 12 dc around 1st leg, 4 dc along ch (32 sts).
25th round: (7 dc, 2 dc in next dc) rep 4 times (36 sts).
26th round: (5 dc, 2 dc in next dc) rep 6 times (42 sts).
27th round: (6 dc, 2 dc in next dc) rep 6 times (48 sts).
28th to 31st rounds: 1 dc in each dc.
32nd round: (10 dc, dec 1 dc) rep 4 times (44 sts).
33rd to 47th round: 1 dc in each dc.
48th round: (1 dc, dec 1 dc) rep 14 times, 2 dc (30 sts).
49th round: (1 dc, dec 1 dc) rep 10 times (20 sts).
50th round: (1 dc, dec 1 dc) rep 6 times, 2 dc (14 sts).
51st to 52nd round: 1 dc in each dc.
Fasten off, leaving long tail for sewing body to head. Stuff body and set aside.

ARMS

Begin with a magic ring.
1st round: 6 dc in magic ring. Pull ends of yarn to tighten ring.
2nd round: 2 dc in each dc (12 sts).
3rd to 21st rounds: 1 dc in each dc. Lightly stuff arm about 3/4 full. Pinch the top of arm together and sl-st closed.
Fasten off, leaving a long tail for sewing.
Make two.

EARS

Begin with a magic ring.
1st round: 4 dc in magic ring. Pull ends of yarn to tighten ring.
2nd round: (1 dc, 2 dc in next dc) rep (6 sts).
3rd round: (1 dc, 2 dc in next dc) rep 3 times (9 sts).
4th round: 1 dc in each dc.
5th round: (1 dc, 2 dc in next dc) rep 3 times, 2 dc (12 sts).
6th round: 1 dc in each dc.
7th round: (3 dc, 2 dc in next dc) rep 3 times (15 sts).
8th to 9th rounds: 1 dc in each dc.
10th round: (3 dc, dec 1 dc) rep 3 times (12 sts).

...THE BIG BAD WOLF

LITTLE Red Riding Hood set off to visit Grandma in smashing knitted gear—boots, pants, striped top, and, of course, a beautiful hooded cape.

BIG Bad Wolf (crocheted in dashing stripes and wearing his red knitted pants) was waiting in the woods. "Hi, Little Red Riding Hood," he whistled, "you look just great."

11th round: 1 dc in each dc. Pinch the ear opening together and sl-st closed.
Fasten off, leaving long tail for attaching to head.
Make two.

TAIL

Ch 25.
1st row: Loop along one side of ch, then back along opposite side.
2nd row: 50 dc along loop sts.
3rd row: Bend pipe-cleaner in half and twist together. Lay it inside tail and enclose using 25 sl-st to join opposite dcs.

OVERALLS

* Cast on 28 sts.
Knit 16 rows in stocking stitch (1 row k, 1 row p).
Cast off 3 sts at beg of next 2 rows (22 sts).
Work 3 more rows. *
Break off yarn, leaving sts on needle. Cast on 2nd leg on same needle and rep * to *.
Next row: Inc 1 st, k 24, inc 1 st, cont on sts of 1st leg, inc 1 st, k 24, inc 1 st (56 sts).
Work 3 rows.
Next row: Inc 1 st at each end (58 sts).
Work 3 rows.
Next row: Inc 1 st at each end (60 sts).
Work 14 rows. Cast off.
Make two straps: Cast on 4 sts, knit 50 rows in stocking stitch. Cast off.

TO MAKE UP

Attach head to body. Sew arms along shoulder line. Attach tail to body. There should be some pipe-cleaner sticking out of end of tail. Use this to stabilise the tail inside the body. Attach ears to head.
Using mattress stitch, sew inside pant legs together. Carefully stitch the crotch (this pulls very easily). Place pants on your wolf and stitch up to the tail. Sew the back seam from the top down to the tail. Attach straps, crossing them over at the back. Attach buttons.
Embroider nose and mouth. You may wish to add eyebrows and white yarn on the outside of the eyes to add character.

Amigurumi

Amigurumi are crocheted stuffed toys or dolls modelled after the *kawaii* (meaning cute) or *chibi* (meaning small) aesthetics originating in Japan. They can be characterised by their larger heads, cute design and the way they are made in a tightly crocheted spiral. The Japanese word 編みぐるみ has two parts: *ami*, meaning crochet or knitted; and *nuigurumu*, meaning stuffed doll. The toys can be modelled after animals, foods and even Disney characters and celebrities. They are often crocheted in separate parts—head, body, arms—and assembled by sewing the parts in place. You need very few materials to get started: yarn, a crochet hook and some suitable stuffing material such as polyester fibre or stuffing beads.

Amigurumi toys as we know them today took off in Japan in the 1970s and 1980s during the *kawaii* movement, which emphasised the 'cutification' of fashion and pop culture characters, like the Hello Kitty franchise. However, crocheted, stuffed dolls were referenced before then in Japanese culture. The oldest known use of the word amigurumi, in the context of crocheted toys, dates from 1951 in a Japanese book titled *Complete Collection of New Handicrafts and Clothing*. The book used amigurumi to refer to various animal characters, and featured patterns and graphics depicting how to create them.

Now, finding patterns to make your own amigurumi is done with ease, with patterns on sale on Etsy and freely available on places like Pinterest and YouTube. It requires few materials, can be inexpensive and enables room for experimentation. The most common crochet techniques you need to know are double crochet, increases, decreases, and single and double loop cast-ons. It is also good to know some embroidery techniques for the eyes and the nose, plus any other embellishments you wish to use—often the most enjoyable element!

Homewares

The earliest crocheted items were homewares such as lacy doilies and antimacassars, so it's no wonder that we're still making crochet projects for our homes.

Retro tableware like our dewdrop doily (page 152), a traditional design reworked in modern colours, is a throwback to classic crochet designs. Your grandmother probably used doilies under vases and ornaments to protect her beautifully polished furniture—there are even stories of women using doilies in their refrigerators!

The motifs of the table runner (page 164) can be worked individually as a doily, or in groups of two or more to make placemats, table runners and even a tablecloth. And we're not finished with the table yet, because there's a gorgeous tea-cosy adorned with a bunch of crochet flowers (see page 168) that will make your teatime special.

While you sip your hot tea, recline on an easy-to-make crochet patchwork cushion (page 160). When you're ready for bed, you can crochet a garland of flowers to sew onto your bedspread (see page 156). These flowers would also look great adorning a cushion, wall-hanging, hat or even your clothing. They're hugely versatile, and a great way of using up scraps of yarn.

Designed for No. 80 mercerised crochet cotton, we've worked this in No. 12 pearl cotton embroidery thread, which has a lovely sheen and comes in hundreds of colours. Three balls are required to make the doily, but we've used four colours, changing at rounds 9, 16 and 24.

You could also use a 4-ply or 8-ply crochet cotton with an appropriately sized hook and make a small round tablecloth. If you're an experienced crocheter, you can add more rounds before round 21 until you reach the size you require.

Intermediate

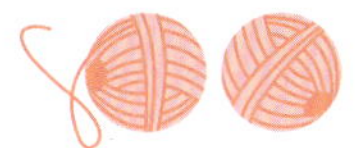

Dewdrop doily

With its pretty lacy edges, this doily will dress up any tabletop.

The Australian Woman's Mirror, 27 June 1951.

Materials: No. 12 pearl cotton, 3 x balls (or 1 x each of 4 colours); 1.25 mm crochet hook.
Measurements: 23 cm in diameter.

DOILY

Commence at centre with a ring of 10 ch.
1st round: 5 ch, 23 dtr into ring, sl-st to 5th of 5 ch.
2nd round: 1 dc between 5 ch and 1st dtr of last round, * 10 ch, 1 dc between next 2 dtr. Rep from * all round, ending with sl-st to 1st dc.
3rd round: Sl-st to centre of loop, 1 dc into loop, * 10 ch, 1 dc into centre of next loop. Rep from * all round, ending with sl-st to dc.
Rep 3rd round 5 times.
9th round: Sl-st to centre of loop, * 10 ch, 1 dc, 3 ch, 1 tr, 1 dc into centre of next loop. Rep from * all round, ending with 10 ch, 1 dc, 3 ch, 1 tr, 1 sl-st into centre of 1st loop.
Rep 9th round twice.
12th round: As 9th round, only work 12 ch instead of 10 ch loops.
Rep 12th round 3 times.
16th round: Sl-st along 8 ch of loop, * 12 ch, 1 dc, 3 ch, 5 tr, 3 ch, 1 dc into centre of next loop. Rep from * all round, ending last rep with sl-st instead of last dc into centre of 1st loop.
Rep 16th round 4 times.
21st round: Sl-st along 8 ch of loop, * 12 ch, 1 dc, 3 ch, 3 tr, 2 ch, 3 dtr, 2 ch, 3 tr, 3 ch, 1 dc into next loop. Rep from * all round, ending last rep with sl-st instead of last dc into 1st loop.
22nd round: Sl-st along 8 ch of loop, * 5 ch, 1 dc into top of 3 ch, 5 ch, 2 tr into next 2 ch, 2 ch, 2 dtr into sp between 1st and 2nd dtr, 2 dtr into sp between 2nd and 3rd dtr, 2 ch, 2 tr into next ch, 5 ch, miss 3 tr, 1 dc into top of 3 ch, 5 ch, 1 dc, 3 ch, 5 tr, 3 ch, 1 dc into next loop. Rep from * all round, ending last rep with sl-st instead of last dc into 1st loop.

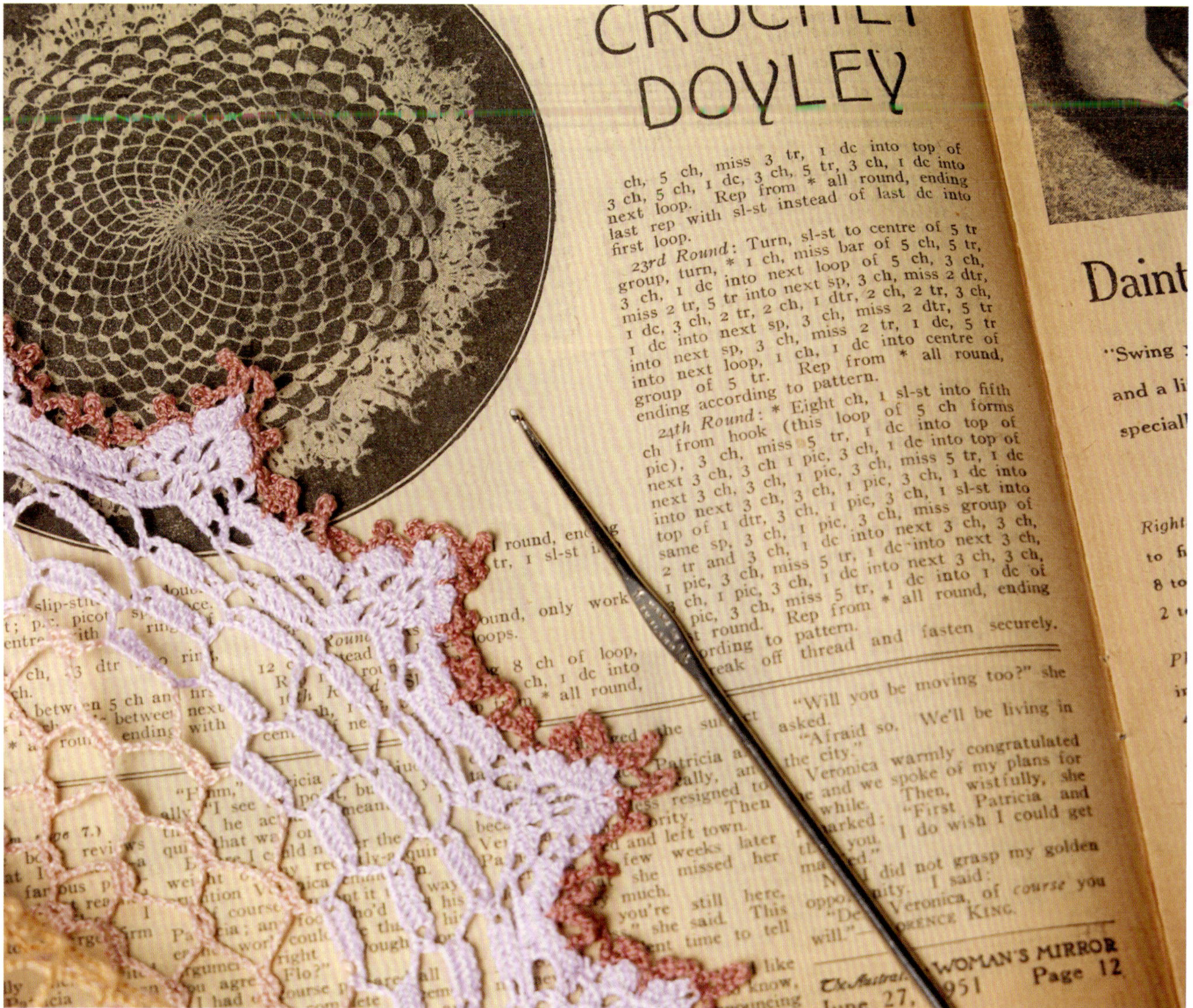

23rd round: Turn, sl-st to centre of 5 tr group, turn, * 1 ch, miss bar of 5 ch, 5 tr, 3 ch, 1 dc into next loop of 5 ch, 3 ch, miss 2 tr, 5 tr into next sp, 3 ch, miss 2 dtr, 1 dc, 3 ch, 2 tr, 2 ch, 1 dtr, 2 ch, 2 tr, 3 ch, 1 dc into next sp, 3 ch, miss 2 dtr, 5 tr into next sp, 3 ch, miss 2 tr, 1 dc, 5 tr into next loop, 1 ch, 1 dc into centre of group of 5 tr. Rep from * all round, ending according to patt.

24th round: * 8 ch, 1 sl-st into 5th ch from hook (this loop of 5 ch forms picot), 3 ch, miss 5 tr, 1 dc into top of next 3 ch, 3 ch, 1 picot, 3 ch, 1 dc into top of next 3 ch, 3 ch, 1 picot, 3 ch, miss 5 tr, 1 dc into next 3 ch, 3 ch, 1 picot, 3 ch, 1 dc into top of 1 dtr, 3 ch, 1 picot, 3 ch, 1 sl-st into same sp, 3 ch, 1 picot, 3 ch, miss group of 2 tr and 3 ch, 1 dc into next 3 ch, 3 ch, 1 picot, 3 ch, miss 5 tr, 1 dc into next 3 ch, 3 ch, 1 picot, 3 ch, 1 dc into next 3 ch, 3 ch, 1 picot, 3 ch, miss 5 tr, 1 dc into 1 dc of last round. Rep from * all round, ending according to patt.
Break off thread and fasten securely.

The D'oyley Show

The D'oyley Show was a 1979 exhibition at Watters Gallery in Sydney by the Women's Domestic Needlework Group. The show presented a history of women's needlework, particularly lace-making, but the Domestic Needlework Group was equally interested in the politics of domestic labour. This was a show with bite, put on at a time when women were arguing for silk, cotton and wool to be treated with the same reverence in the art world as marble, wood, clay and metals.

The exhibition displayed doilies dating from the seventeenth century through to 1979, grouped by theme or crochet type or purpose. There were roses and shamrocks in Irish crochet lace; linen doilies with embroidered Australian flora and crochet edging; parrots, cats, teapots, the Sydney Harbour Bridge and everything in between. There were messages supporting peace, war, temperence and the monarchy, as well as gender equality and social justice.

A series of ten posters in The D'oyley Show, and now in the collections of the National Library of Australia, includes 'The song of the skirt', 'Women who toiled' and 'Fancywork the archaeology of lives'. The posters show historic images of women engaging in textile work and celebrate women's creativity and industry captioned with subversive sentiments like 'the artist imprisoned in the housewife' and 'the dye for the rose-coloured tulle, girls, is our blood'.

Although this design may appear elaborate, it is not difficult to work, as all the flowers are separately crocheted and may be made in odd moments. An advantage is that scraps of different colour wools may be used.

On some of the flat round flowers work a few black French knots around the centre. The original design was to be sewn onto a bedspread made of gold filet net. Use the flowers in any way you like!

Beginner

Decorative garland

All the bright colours of a summer garden are blended together to create this floral design.

The Australian Home Beautiful, 1 December 1933.

Materials: Small quantities of yarn in as many colours as you like. We used 4-ply acrylic yarn and a 2.25 mm crochet hook.

Notes: Crochet over the starting tail as you make each flower centre, and use it to pull the ring tight after the 1st round.

Leave yarn tails long for sewing or tying flowers to the backing fabric.

Begin rounds with chain, counting as 1st stitch; for example, 2 ch for dc, 3 ch for tr, 4 ch for dtr, and at end of round sl-st into top chain to join.

FLOWER 1

1st round: Make 8 ch, sl-st to join in a ring.
2nd round: 25 tr into ring.
3rd round: 25 dtr with 1 ch between each.
4th round: 3 ch, 1 dc into every alternate dtr.

FLOWER 2

1st round: Make 10 ch, join in a ring.
2nd round: 16 tr into ring.
3rd round: 1 dc, 5 ch, 1 dc into secnd tr. Make 8 loops.
4th round: 1 dc, 4 ch, 3 tr, 4 ch, 1 dc into each loop. Make 8 petals all together.
To finish: Make Flower 5 and sew on to Flower 2 to form centre.

FLOWER 3

For centre of flower.
1st round: Make 5 ch, join in a ring.
2nd round: 10 dc into ring.
3rd round: 15 dc into prev row.
4th round: 20 dc into prev row.
5th round: 30 dc into prev row.
Join on contrast colour wool. 12 ch, 1 tr into 2nd ch from end, 9 tr into each ch to end, 1 ch into 3rd dc, sl-st into 3rd dc. Rep to make 7 petals altogether. These petals curl up and are sewn to the centre.

FLOWER 4

1st round: Make 8 ch, join in a ring.
2nd round: 16 tr into the ring.
3rd round: 2 ch, 1 dc into every tr to form loops around flower.

FLOWER 5

1st round: 8 ch, join in a ring.
2nd round: 4 ch, 3 dtr, 4 ch, dc into ring. Rep 4 times to form 5 petals.
To finish: In contrast colours ch 4, fill in ring with dc, add secnd row of dc. Fasten off, leaving a long tail to sew centre to flower.

FLOWER 6

1st round: The same as Flower 5, only make 6 petals.
To finish: In contrast colours ch 4, fill in ring with dc, add 2nd row of dc. Fasten off, leaving a long tail to sew centre to flower.

FLOWER 7

1st round: In green yarn, ch 4.
2nd round: 8 tr into 4 ch.
3rd round: Change to another colour yarn, work 16 tr into the 8 tr of prev row.
4th round: 1 dc into each tr.

BUDS AND STEMS

Using green yarn, ch 9, 5 tr into last ch, sl-st back along ch, then make 7 ch, 5 tr into last ch, sl-st back along the ch to the join. Make 7 ch, 5 tr into last ch, sl-st back to the join. This makes 3 stems and the bases of the buds. Join coloured yarn on to green bud, make 7 tr to form the flower bud. Rep for 2 other buds.

LEAVES

In green yarn, make 10 ch, miss 1 ch, 1 dc into next ch, 1 dtr into next 5 ch, 1 tr, 1 dc, sl-st to fasten off.
To make a larger leaf, commence with 16 ch, miss 1 ch, 1 dc, 1 dtr into next 11 ch, 1 tr, 1 dc, sl-st to fasten off.

TO MAKE UP

Arrange flowers as desired on backing and use the tails of yarn to sew them on. Alternatively, finish off tails neatly and use a hot-glue gun to attach flowers to the surface with a dab of hot glue behind the centres.

A NOVELTY IN BED
A Gay Garland of Crochet Woolflowers on a
By IVY RUSSELL
ALL the bright colors of a summer garden are blended together to create this floral design. Unfortunately no idea of its brilliance can be obtained from a plain photograph. Leaves of crochet in two shades of green, with touches of black in the centres of the flowers add to the effect.
Although this design may appear elaborate, it is not difficult to work, as all the flowers are separately crocheted and may be made in odd moments. An added advantage is that scraps of different colored wools may be utilised.
All shades of mauve, pink, blue, orange, yellow, petunia, red, buttercup and white may be used.
A petunia centre looks attractive on a blue flower.
On some of the flat round flowers work a few black French knots around the d.c. centre.
The spread is made of nine yards of 36in. gold filet net cut
DIRECTIONS FOR WORKING

Beginner

Patchwork cushion

Straight lines and easy-to-follow instructions make this a fun décor project for a beginner crocheter.

The Australian Woman's Mirror, 28 March 1939.

Materials: 8-ply cotton yarn, 100 g balls: 1 x each of 3 colours (C1, C2, C3); 3.50 mm crochet hook; 50 cm square plain fabric cushion cover (or make your own); 50 cm square cushion insert.

Measurements: To fit 50 cm square cushion. Finished crochet work is about 47 cm square and must be blocked to shape and sewn onto the cushion.

Special stitches: The cushion is in dc (double crochet), always working into back loop of stitch to form a ribbed effect.

CUSHION

1st row: Into a ring of 5 ch, work 3 dc. Turn at end of this and every row with 1 ch.

2nd row: 1 dc into 1st dc, 3 dc into next, 1 dc into last.

3rd and following rows: 1 dc into each dc up to centre dc of row. Into centre dc work 3 dc, then 1 dc into each remaining dc of row. There is no need to count stitches, just watch for centre dc which is over hole of prev row.

Use the colours as follows: C1 until you have 13 ribs, C2 for 11 ribs, then C3 for 9 ribs. Fasten off. Make another piece the same. Work two more pieces with the colours reversed: that is, C3 for 13 ribs, C2 for 11 ribs, C1 for 9 ribs.

TASSEL

To make a cup: Make a ring of 5 ch and work 6 dc into ring.

1st row: 1 dc into each dc.

2nd row: Work 2 dc into every 2nd dc (9 dc).

3rd to 6th rows: 1 dc into each dc.

7th row: 1 single crochet into each dc. Fasten off.

To make the tassel: Wind remaining yarn around a 27 cm piece of heavy cardboard. Tie together at one edge, then press under a cloth, cut at other edge of cardboard. Pull tied end of tassel into cup and pass tie ends through the centre hole, ready to sew on to cushion.

The original pattern suggested crepe silk or 3-ply wool, but we chose a sturdy 8-ply cotton, which is often available in colours to match your décor.

TO MAKE UP

Sew the four pieces together so that opposite corners match. The work will not be flat when joined, but is pressed into shape as follows: place right-side down on a towel. Pin down at seams, then use plenty of pins and stretch remaining rows until work is square. Place a damp cloth over and press with a hot iron until dry. Using this method, the cushion will not sag.
Sew the tassel to the centre of the cushion, then sew the crochet to the front of the cushion around all edges.

Luminaries of lace-making

> *Crochet, with the exception of the Irish School, has hitherto held a very humble, not to say despised! position as a lace, though it has been popular for useful woollen articles and for decorating linen, etc. But now the little hook has entered the lists ! and those who avail themselves of the present opportunity will, perhaps, be surprised at its achievements.*

Margaret Ann Field, aka Mrs Edwin Field, aka 'A Briton Beyond the Seas', was a textile artist, fashion designer and amateur astronomer. She published *Australian Lace-Crochet* in February of 1909, the result, she wrote, of 45 years of honing her craft.

Her married life in Australia, following her engineer husband around remote parts of the country, was one of privation and isolation. She crocheted and observed the stars to fill her evenings when her children were sleeping. Developing her 'Australian Lace-Crochet', which she considered easier than Irish Crochet, became a focus because she missed 'the beautiful things' she had grown up with in her native Scotland. Her patterns combined her interests in astronomy and her talents with a crochet hook, with each named after a constellation.

It was in a very different landscape that women had first used a crochet hook to make lace. In the mid-1800s, peasant women in Ireland adopted the craft as a way to earn money during the Great Famine. In Australia, the association of Irish lace with a peasant class persisted, even as many pioneer women adopted the craft, using it to decorate clothes and household items. Field's pattern book, commended by Queen Alexandra, was published during one of lace crochet's periodic revivals, and original designs, often featuring Australian flora, were beginning to appear in magazines and on display at agricultural shows.

In the same decade, a deaf Mary Card turned her hand to crochet lace design. Needing a source of income, Card set her mind to becoming proficient in crochet-work. She submitted an early pattern to America's *Ladies' Home Journal*, and this began a thirty-year international career. She was a superstar of crochet design, appearing in the media, providing celebrity product endorsements and acquiring a loyal readership in Australia, America and England.

Today the works of both women are held in the collections of Australia's leading cultural institutions, including the Powerhouse Museum, the National Gallery of Victoria and the National Gallery of Australia.

Margaret Field made this Irish crochet square as a cushion sham sometime prior to 1909.

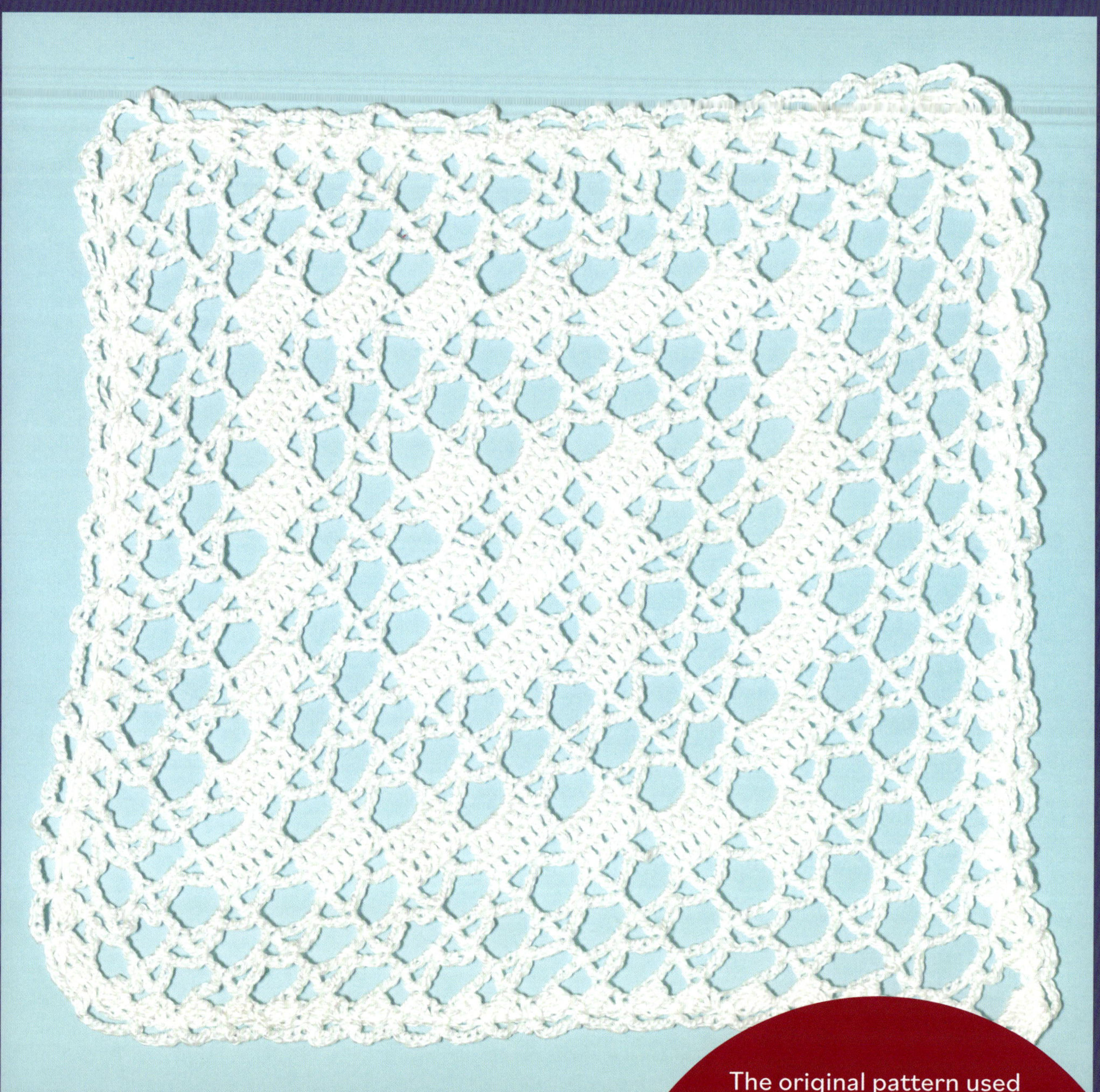

The original pattern used No. 40 crochet cotton (approximately equivalent to a No. 12 pearl cotton) and a 1.75 mm steel hook for a light, lacy effect. Our sample was worked in 2-ply satin-finish crochet cotton using a 2 mm hook, which resulted in a larger square suitable for use on its own as a doily. You could use any cotton yarn with an appropriate sized hook. Make as many squares as you like and join them to create a placemat, tablecloth or even a bedspread.

Intermediate

Mosaic table runner

Each motif square used in this project is worked diagonally from corner to corner.

The Australian Woman's Mirror, 26 November 1947.

Materials: Option 1: 2-ply satin crochet cotton (No. 5 pearl), 50 g ball; 2.00 mm crochet hook. Option 2: No. 40 crochet cotton, 4 x 20 g balls; 1.75 mm steel crochet hook.

Measurements: Our sample in modern 2-ply satin-finish crochet cotton measures 25 cm square. Each mosaic square in No. 40 crochet cotton measures 13.5 cm square. A table runner of 3 x 7 squares in No. 40 would measure 40 cm x 93.5 cm.

Special stitches: Diagonal block (diag blk): 4 tr into same sp (turning ch counts as 1st tr at beg of row); Lacet (lac): 3 ch, miss 2 tr, dc, 3 ch, miss 2 tr.

MOTIF

Starting at lower corner, commence with 5 ch.

1st row: 6 tr into 5th ch from hook, 4 ch, turn.

2nd row: 3 tr at base of turning ch (a diag blk increased), 3 ch, miss 2 tr, 1 dc into next tr, 3 ch, miss 2 tr, 4 tr into 4th of 4 ch prev row (a lac completed and another diag blk increased), 4 ch, turn.

3rd row: Inc a diag blk as before, 2 ch, miss 2 tr, 1 tr into next tr (sp made over blk), 5 ch, 1 tr into next tr (a bar made), 2 ch, miss 2 tr, 4 tr into top of turning ch (another sp made and another diag blk increased), 4 ch, turn.

4th row: Inc a diag blk as before, 3 ch, miss 2 tr, 1 dc into next tr, 3 ch, miss next sp, 1 tr into next tr (a lac made), 3 ch, 1 dc over bar of 5 ch, 3 ch, 1 tr into next tr (another lac made), 3 ch, 1 dc into next tr, 3 ch, miss 2 tr, 4 tr into 4th of turning ch (another lac completed and a diag blk increased), 4 ch, turn.

Continue working in this manner, following diagram until 7th row is completed, ending with 4 ch, turn.

8th row: Inc a diag blk as before, 3 lac, 5 tr into next sp of 5 ch, 1 tr into next tr (a large blk made), 3 lac and inc a diag blk at end of row as before, 4 ch, turn.
9th row: Inc a diag blk as before, 2 ch, miss 2 sts, 1 tr into next tr (sp made), 3 bars, 1 tr into each of the next 6 tr (another large blk made), 3 bars, 1 sp, inc a diag blk at end of row as before, 4 ch, turn.
Now follow image on page 164 until 19 rows have been completed, ending with 4 ch, turn.
(To make lac over large blk, work 3 ch, miss 3 tr, 1 dc into next tr, 3 ch, miss 2 tr, 1 tr into next tr)
20th row: Inc a diag blk, 3 lac, 1 large blk, 3 lac, 1 large blk, 2 sps, (2 tr into next sp, 1 tr into next tr) twice (another large blk made), and follow image across, 4 ch, turn.
21st row: 1 tr into each of the next 3 tr, holding back on hook the last loop of each tr, thread over and draw through all loops on hook (1 blk dec), 3 bars, 1 large blk and follow image across row, ending with 3 bars, 5 ch.
Now, holding back the last loop of each st, 1 tr into each of the next 3 tr and in top st of turning ch, thread over and draw all loops on hook (another blk decreased), 4 ch, turn.
22nd row: 1 tr into each of the next 3 sts, holding back on hook the last loop of each tr, thread over and draw through all loops on hook (a dec made), 2 ch, 1 tr into next tr and follow image across, ending with 2 ch.
Holding back on hook the last loop of each st, work 1 tr into each of the last 3 sts and in tip of decreased blk below, thread over and draw through all loops on hook (another dec made), 4 ch, turn.
Cont working in this manner, following image to within last row, 4 ch, turn.
Last row: Holding back on hook the last loop of each st, work 5 tr in next 5 ch, sp and 1 tr at tip of next dec blk, thread over and draw through all loops on hook. Do not fasten off, but work loops around outer edges of square as follows.
Loop round: * 5 ch, 1 dc at top of decreased blk of prev row. Rep from * to within corner, 5 ch, 2 dc into corner and continue thus, making 5 ch loops all round, each loop covering 1 row, ending with 5 ch, 1 sl-st at base of 5 ch first made (20 loops on each side of square).
Fasten off. Dampen and block out to desired measurements.

TABLE RUNNER

Work 2nd motif as for 1st motif to within the loop round.
Loop round: 2 ch, 1 dc into corresponding loop of 1st motif, 2 ch, 1 dc at tip of decreased blk below on motif in work, and continue as for 1st motif, joining all loops of adjacent sides as before.
Make necessary number of motifs, joining adjacent sides in the same way as 2nd motif was joined to 1st motif.
Dampen and block out to desired measurements.

Designed for the MIRROR by a COATS-CLARK Needlework Expert.

A MOSAIC PATTERN TABLE RUNNER

USE for this runner made up of 21 linked crochet squares in a mosaic design 4 balls (20 gram) of Coats's mercer-crochet No. 40 in any selected color, and a No. 4 steel crochet hook. (Tight workers could use a No. 3½ hook, and slack workers a No. 4½.)

Tension: 5¼in. (13.5cm.) square.

Measurements: 15¾in. (40cm.) x 36¾in. (93.5cm.), 3 motifs x 7 motifs.

Abbreviations: Ch, chain; dc, double crochet; tr, treble; inc, increase; sp, space; blk, block; ss, slip-stitch; sts, stitches; dec, decrease; diag, diagonal; lac, lacet; con, continue; lp, loop; rep, repeat.

FIRST MOTIF.—Starting at lower point on diagram (photo of square, top of page), commence with 5 ch.

1st Row: 6 tr into 5th ch from hook, 4 ch, turn.

2nd Row: 3 tr at base of turning ch (a diag blk increased), 3 ch, miss 2 tr, 1 dc into next tr, 3 ch, miss 2 tr, 4 tr into 4th of 4 ch of previous row (a lacet completed and another diag blk increased), 4 ch, turn.

3rd Row: Inc a diag blk as before, 2 ch, miss 2 tr, 1 tr into next tr (sp made over blk), 5 ch, 1 tr into next tr (a bar made), 2 ch, miss 2 tr, 4 tr into top of turning ch (another sp made and another diag blk increased), 4 ch, turn.

4th Row: Inc a diag blk as before, 3 ch, miss 2 tr, 1 dc into next tr, 3 ch, miss next sp, 1 tr into next tr (a lac made), 3 ch, 1 dc over bar of 5 ch, 3 ch, 1 tr into next tr (another lac made), 3 ch, 1 dc into next tr, 3 ch, miss 2 tr, 4 tr into 4th of turning ch (another lac completed and a diag blk increased), 4 ch, turn.

Con working in this manner, following diagram until 7th row is completed, ending with 4 ch, turn.

8th Row: Inc a diag blk as before, 3 lac, 5 tr into next sp of 5 ch, 1 tr into next tr (a large blk made), 3 lac and inc a diag blk at end of row as before, 4 ch, turn.

9th Row: Inc a diag blk as before, 2 ch, miss 2 sts, 1 tr into next tr (sp made), 3 bars, 1 tr into each of the next 6 tr (another large blk made), 3 bars, 1 sp, inc a diag blk at end of row as before, 4 ch, turn.

Now follow diagram until 19 rows have been completed, ending with 4 ch, turn. (To make lac over large blks work 3 ch, miss 2 tr, 1 dc into next tr, 3 ch, miss 2 tr, 1 tr into next tr.)

20th Row: Inc a diag blk, 3 lac, 1 large blk, 3 lac, 1 large blk, 2 sps, (2 tr into next sp, 1 tr into next tr) twice (another large blk made), and follow diagram across, 4 ch, turn.

21st Row: 1 tr into each of the next 3 tr, holding back on hook the last lp of each tr, thread over and draw through all lps on hook (1 blk decreased), 3 bars, 1 large blk and follow diagram across row, ending with 2 bars, 5 ch.

Now, holding back on hook the last lp of each st, 1 tr into each of the next 3 tr and in top st of turning ch, thread over and draw through all lps on hook (another blk decreased), 4 ch, turn.

22nd Row: 1 tr into each of the next 3 sts, holding back on hook the last lp of each tr, thread over and draw through all lps on hook (a dec made), 2 ch, 1 tr into next tr and follow diagram across, ending with 2 ch.

Holding back on hook the last lp of each st, work 1 tr into each of the last 3 sts and in tip of decreased blk below, thread over and draw through all lps on hook (another dec made), 4 ch, turn.

Con working in this manner, following diagram to within the last row, 4 ch, turn.

Last Row: Holding back on hook the last lp of each st, work 5 tr in next 5 ch, sp and 1 tr at tip of next decreased blk, thread

(Continued on page 29.)

Intermediate

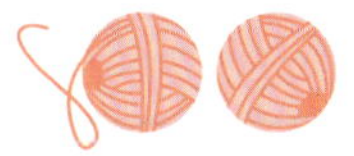

Flower tea-cosy

Designed for *The Australian Woman's Mirror* in the midst of the Second World War, the editors thought this would make a delightful (and no doubt budget-friendly) Christmas gift.

The Australian Woman's Mirror, 7 December 1943.

Materials: 4-ply wool yarn, 50 g balls: 1 x main colour (MC), small amounts of various colours for the flowers; 3.00 mm crochet hook.
Measurements: Finished cosy measures 11 cm high by 16 cm wide.

TEA-COSY

1st round: Commence with 12 ch ring.
2nd round: 4 ch to form 1st tr, 31 tr into ring.
3rd round: 4 ch, * 2 tr into 2 tr, 2 tr into next tr. Rep from * to end of round.
4th round: 4 ch, * 2 tr into next tr, 1 tr into next tr. Rep from * to end of round.
5th and 6th rounds: Rep 4th round.
7th, 8th and 9th rounds: 1 tr into each tr of prev round.
10th round: 4 ch, 1 tr into 1st tr, * miss 1 tr, 2 tr into next tr. Rep from * half-way round.
11th round: Turn, 4 ch, 1 tr into middle of 1st 2 tr, * 2 tr into middle of next 2 tr. Rep from * to end of row.
Rep 8 rows.
Work other side in same manner for 9 rows.
On the 10th row work all round.
Continue for 4 more rounds. Finish with 4 rounds of dc.

FLOWER

With centre colour, 6 ch ring, 12 dc into ring, join, break off wool.
With petal colour, 1 dc into 1st dc, * 6 tr into next dc, 1 dc into next dc. Rep from * 5 times, leaving long tail with which to attach flower to cosy.
Make about 40 flowers.

The original cosy was in 2-ply yarn which we judged to be closer to modern 4-ply. It fits a small teapot. If your teapot is larger, work extra increase rows in the beginning to make it bigger before dividing for the spout and handle. Try the cosy on your pot as you work to ensure that it fits.

BASKET OF FLOWERS TEACOSY

Designed for the MIRROR *by* H AMU.

A CHRISTMAS GIFT IDEA

MADE of two-ply, this basket of flowers tea cosy requires two ounces of the wool, using a bone crochet hook size 12.

Abbreviations: Ch, chain; tr, treble; rep, repeat; dc, double crochet.

1st Round: Commence 7 ch ring.

2nd Round: Four ch to form first tr, 31 tr into ring.

3rd Round: Four ch, * 2 tr into 2 tr, 2 tr into next tr. Rep from * to end of round.

4th Round: Four ch, * 2 tr into next tr, 1 tr into next tr. Rep from * to end of round.

5th and 6th Rounds: Rep fourth round.

7th, 8th and 9th Rounds: One tr into each tr of previous round.

10th Round: Four ch, 1 tr into first tr, * miss 1 tr, 2 tr into next tr. Rep from * halfway round.

11th Round: Turn, 4 ch, 1 tr into middle of first 2 tr, * 2 tr into middle of next 2 tr. Rep from * to end of row.

Rep eight rows.

Work other side in same manner for nine rows.

On the tenth row work all round.

Continue for four more rounds.

Finish with four rounds of dc.

A FLOWER.—With dark-blue wool for centre, 6 ch ring, 12 dc into ring, join, break off wool.

With light-blue wool 1 dc into first dc, * 6 tr into next dc, 1 dc into next dc. Rep from * 5 times, leaving length of wool with which to attach flower to cosy.

LINK HANDLES.—Wind wool 18 times over three fingers, 41 dc over wool, join and break off thread.

LINK HANDLES

Wind yarn 18 times over three fingers, 41 dc over yarn, sl-st to join and break off thread.

2nd link: Pass wool through 1st link and over one finger 18 times, 36 dc over wool, join.

TO MAKE UP

Attach link handles. Sew flowers on top of cosy in a pleasing arrangement.

References

Alder, Alison, 'Frances (Budden) Phoenix', excerpted from *Know My Name* (NGA, 2020), National Gallery of Australia, nga.gov.au/knowmyname/artists/frances-budden-phoenix/

Ballantyne, Barbara, *Mary Card: Australian Crochet Lace Designer*, Drummoyne (NSW): B. Ballantyne, 2002

'Barntröja [Child's Sweater]', *Penelope: The Newest Women's Journal: Album for Feminine Activity and Concerns* (Sweden), 1857, pp.189–190

Cochrane, Grace, *The Crafts Movement in Australia: A History*, Kensington (NSW): NSW University Press, 1992

Craft Australia, Sydney: Crafts Council of Australia, 1971–1988

'Crochet Coral Reef', crochetcoralreef.org

'DIY Definitions: Amigurumi', DIY Life, web.archive.org/web/20090126185126/diylife.com/2007/08/07/diy-definitions-amigurumi-with-tutorial/

The D'oyley Show: An Exhibition of Women's Domestic Fancywork, Sydney: D'oyley Publications, 1979

Esa, Jessica, 'Amigurumi: All You Need to Know about Japanese Crochet', Japan Objects, japanobjects.com/features/amigurumi

'Evelyn Roth', Evelyn Roth Arts, evelynrotharts.com/evelynroth

Field, Mrs Edwin, *Australian Lace-crochet: Easy and Artistic / by a Briton beyond the Seas*, London: Simpkin, Marshall, Hamilton, Kent & Co., 1909

Ford, Eleanor, 'Plarn Crochet Baskets', Mini Mad Things, minimadthings.com/blogs/news/plarn-crochet-baskets

'Gehäkeltes Tuch [Crocheted Scarf]', *The Bazaar: Berlin Illustrated Women's Magazine* (Prussia), vol.8, issue 2, 1858, pp.11–12

'Housewife Superstar' and Author Marjorie Bligh Dies at 96', *ABC News*, abc.net.au/ news/2013-09-25/housewife-icon-and-author-marjorie-bligh-dies-at-96/4980346

Isaacs, Jennifer, *The Gentle Arts: 200 Years of Australian Women's Domestic and Decorative Arts*, Sydney: Landsdowne, 1987

Karp, Cary, 'Defining Crochet, Textile History', *Textile History*, vol.49, issue 2, 2018, pp.208–223

Karp, Cary, 'The Princess, Frederick William Stitch: The Parallel Emergence of Long-Hook Crochet in Prussia and England in 1858', *The Journal of Dress History*, vol.4, issue 2, 2020, pp.75–112

Killian, Lara, 'Getting Started with Knitting & Crocheting in the Library', *YA Hotline*, no.89, 2010

'The Ladies' Column', *Weekly Times* (Melbourne), 15 April 1871, p.14, nla.gov.au/newspaper/article/219369106

Lampkin, Veronica, 'Mining the Archive: An Historical Study of Madame Weigel's Paper Patterns and Their Relationship to the Fashion and Clothing Needs of Colonial Australasia during the Period 1877 to 1910', PhD thesis, Griffith University, 2013, research-repository.griffith.edu.au/handle/10072/366083

McPhee, John, *Australian Decorative Arts in the Australian National Gallery*, Canberra: ANG, 1982

Mee, Cornelia and Austin, Mary, *Crochet à la Tricoter*, series 1, London: Aylott and Son, 1858

Middendorf, Melissa, 'Amigurumi', *Cincinnati Examiner* (USA), 25 April 2009, infoweb.newsbank.com/apps/news/document-view?p=AWGLNB&docref=news/1341FE40F428FB48

Ngai, Natalie, 'Sugar and Spice (and Everything Nice?): Japan's Ambition behind Lolita's Kawaii Aesthetics', *Media, Culture & Society*, vol.45, no.3, 2023, pp.545–560

'Of Interest to Women', *Narandera Argus and Riverina Advertiser* (NSW), 29 March 1940, p.6, nla.gov.au/nla.news-article130460975

'Old Man Has Crochet Entry', *The Biz* (Fairfield, NSW), 7 December 1960, p.11, nla.gov.au/nla.news-article190737235

Pearlman, Jonathan, 'Inspiration for Dame Edna' Marjorie Bligh Dies Aged 96', *The Telegraph* (United Kingdom), telegraph.co.uk/news/worldnews/australiaandthepacific/australia/1033 2641/Inspiration-for-Dame-Edna-Marjorie-Bligh-dies-aged-96.html

'Phoenix Rising: The Frances (Budden) Phoenix Collection', The Women's Library, thewomenslibrary.org.au/phoenix-rising-the-frances-budden-phoenix-collection

'Pillow Sham with Wattle and Blue Wren Motifs Designed by Mary Card', Powerhouse Collection, collection.powerhouse.com.au/object/112153

Prose, Elizabeth, 'On the Mend: Victorian Rehabilitation with Crochet Granny Squares', *Piecework Magazine*, pieceworkmagazine.com/mend-victorian-rehabilitation-crochet-granny-squares/

Pullan, Matilda Marian, *The Lady's Manual of Fancy Work*, 1858, p.43

Ramirez Saldarriaga, Jennifer, 'Amigurumi', Masters thesis, Aalto University, 2016, urn.fi/URN:NBN:fi:aalto-201610124866

Shane, Janelle, 'First There Was SkyKnit. Now There's HAT3000', *AI Weirdness*, https://www.aiweirdness.com/first-there-was-skyknit-now-theres-19-09-04/

Sheikh, Rehmetullah, 'Artist Crochets Video Tapes into Sculptures to Give Plastic Waste New Life, Play with Media', *CBC News*, cbc.ca/news/canada/british-columbia/artist-crochets-vhs-tapes-recycling-1.5194999

'Show Exhibits of Crochet Work Entered by Retired Cleric', *The Australian Women's Weekly*, 1 April 1953, p.23, nla.gov.au/nla.news-article40465708

'Tasmanian Domestic Goddess Marjorie Bligh', Council of Australasian Museum Directors, camd.org.au/tasmanian-domestic-goddess-marjorie-bligh

Toy, Ann (et al.), *Hearth and Home: Women's Decorative Arts and Crafts 1800–1930*, Glebe (NSW): Historic Houses Trust of New South Wales, 1988

'Trevor Smith: A Fanciful Feast', Art Gallery of Ballarat, artgalleryofballarat.com.au/explore/exhibitions/trevor-smith-a-fanciful-feast

'The Victorian Exhibition of 1875', *The Argus* (Melbourne), 3 September 1875, p.1, nla.gov.au/nla.news-article11523124

White, Sarah, 'How to Make Plarn', The Spruce Crafts, thesprucecrafts.com/how-to-make-plarn-2117354

White, Sarah, 'How to Make T-Shirt Yarn', The Spruce Crafts, thesprucecrafts.com/how-to-make-t-shirt-yarn-2117355

'Women's Work', *The Sun* (Sydney), 31 March 1915, p.5, nla.gov.au/nla.news-article229332154

'The World's First Granny Square Pattern (Plus 7 More to Make)', The Yarn Queen, 2022, theyarnqueen.co.nz/worlds-first-granny-square-pattern/

List of Illustrations

The photographs on the following pages were taken by Lindi Heap and Claire Williams, National Library of Australia: front cover, ends, 1–3, 12, 15, 18, 20, 23, 25–26, 28, 30–31, 33–35, 39, 41–42, 44, 46, 49, 51, 53, 55–56, 59, 61, 63, 65, 67–68, 72, 77,79–80, 83–84, 87–88, 91, 94, 99–102, 104, 106, 109–110, 112, 115–116, 118, 122, 125–126, 128, 130, 134, 136–139, 141, 143–144, 147, 150, 154, 156, 159, 161–162, 164, 169, 171, 173, 175, back cover.

6 Illustration between pages 90–91 in *Penélopé, of maandwerk aan het vrouwelijk geslacht toegewijd* by A.B. Van Meerten (Amsterdam; G.J.A. Beijerinck, 1823); **16** Cover of *The Australian Woman's Mirror*, 9 June 1954, nla.obj-480286263; **19** Illustration from *The Prairie Farmer*, 4 April 1885, Illinois Digital Newspaper Collections; **27** *Photo Taken in the Exhibition 'Wie Schönes Wissen schafft' at Tübingen*, 2013, commons.wikimedia.org/wiki/File:The_F%C3%B6hr_Reef_in_T%C3%BCbingen.jpg; **37** Madam Weigel Pty. Ltd, *Cushions and Cosies*, (Richmond, Vic; Madame Weigel Pty Ltd, 1930), nla.cat-vn2115908; **45** 'Head-lines for Winter', page 75 in *The Australian Women's Weekly*, 19 April 1967, nla.news-page4976699; **57** Courtesy Alex Woolner, attackbearpress.com; **60** Image in 'Bikini Plus', page 33 in *The Australian Women's Weekly*, 23 January 1974, nla.news-page4807937; **69** Image in 'Snazzy Sun-top to Crochet', page 49 in *The Australian Women's Weekly*, 9 October 1974, nla.news-page4890269; **70** Ewa Pachucka, *Arcadia: Landscape and Bodies* 1972–77 (detail), Art Gallery of New South Wales, gift of Rudy Komon Art Gallery 1978 © Estate of Ewa Pachucka, image © Art Gallery of New South Wales; **71 (top):** Frances (Budden) Phoenix, *Get Your Abortion Laws Off Our Bodies*, 1980, Collection of the Estate of the artist; **71 (bottom):** Trevor Smith, *Pig's Head Platter*, 2022, 2022.69, Collection of the Art Gallery of Ballarat; **74** Image in 'Crochet Arrowhead Rib Pullover', page 6 in *The Australian Woman's Mirror*, 15 September 1948, nla.obj-484825278; **78** Image in 'Rainbow-hued Jacket in Crochet', page 21 in *The Australian Women's Weekly*, 20 May 1944, nla.news-page4726406; **82** Image in 'Poncho Skirt and Cap', page 11 in *The Australian Women's Weekly*, 17 March 1971, nla.news-page4888282; **87** Cover of *The Australian Woman's Mirror*, 15 July 1953, nla.obj-496202749; **92** Evelyn Roth, *TV Trap*, c.1974, Courtesy Evelyn Roth; **93** Evelyn Roth, *Video Armour*, 1972, Courtesy Evelyn Roth; **96** Image in 'A Pochette in Crochet', page 30 in *The Australian Woman's Mirror*, 17 March 1931, nla.obj-418990637; **97** The Queen's Scarf, A04279, image courtesy Australian War Memorial; **102** Images in 'Mod Collars to Crochet', page 81 in *The Australian Women's Weekly*, 10 November 1965, nla.news-page4919695; **106** Images in 'Teach Yourself to Crochet and Knit', page 39 in *The Australian Women's Weekly*, 10 June 1970, nla.news-page5341876; **107** Image in 'Show Exhibits of Crochet Work Entered by Retired Cleric', *The Australian Women's Weekly*, 1953, p.23, nla.news-page4382271; **111** 'Crochet Yourself a Shopping Carry-all', page 40 in *The Australian Woman's Mirror*, 3 January 1951, nla.obj-564105222; **117** Image in 'Baby Dazzlers', page 29 in *The Australian Women's Weekly*, 20 September 1972, nla.news-page5344758; **120** 'Crochet These Novelties', page 27 in *The Australian Woman's Mirror*, 25 August 1936, nla.obj-419383302; **121** seramo, *Tunisian Crochet Striped Background Stock Photo*, istockphoto.com/photo/tunisian-crochet-striped-background-gm937399854-256410351; **124** Header in 'The

Work Table', page 8 in *The Colonist*, 14 April 1888, nla.news-article201177560; **129** 'Fete Specials to Sew, Knit or Crochet', page 11 in *The Australian Women's Weekly*, 20 September 1978, nla.news-page5841683; **132** 'Crochet Jumper for Toddler', page 6 in *The Australian Woman's Mirror*, 21 March 1944, nla.obj-566621014; **133** N. Neuen, *Learning Finger Crochet*, 2012, flickr.com/photos/32109672@N04/7723593084/in/photostream/; **139** Image in 'Mad Caps', page 114 in *The Australian Women's Weekly*, 5 April 1978, nla.news-page5843353; **142** 'Quick to Crochet Holiday Togs', page 34 in *The Australian Women's Weekly*, 24 January 1973, nla.news-page5795053; **147** Image in 'Fairytale Toys in Knitting and Crochet', page 33 in *The Australian Women's Weekly*, 17 May 1972, nla.news-page4886845; **148** hiphotos35, *Soft Knitted Toy on White Background*, 2018, istockphoto.com/photo/soft-knitted-toy-and-on-white-background-gm1080007000-289454774; **149** Edwina Grandas, *Amigurumi Sushi*, 2022, istockphoto.com/photo/delicious-and-fresh-set-of-traditional-japanese-nigiri-sushi-handmade-in-crochet-and-gm1402998721-455709946; **155 (left)** Women's Domestic Needlework Group, *Fancywork the Archaeology of Lives*, 1979, nla.cat-vn5016709; **155 (right)** Women's Domestic Needlework Group, *Song of the Skirt*, 1979, nla.cat-vn5016709; **158** Image in 'A Novelty in Bed Spread Designs', page 50 in *The Australian Woman's Mirror*, 1 December 1933, nla.obj-2978404930; **162** Image in 'Patchwork Cushion in Crochet', page 22 in *The Australian Woman's Mirror*, 28 March 1939; **163** Margaret Ann Field, *Lace Crochet Made by Margaret Ann Field*, c.1900–1920, Powerhouse Collection. Gift of Mrs Lee Bryne, 1988. Photo: Russell Perkins; **67** 'A Mosaic Pattern Table Runner', page 16 in *The Australian Woman's Mirror*, 26 November 1924, nla.obj-509126446; **170** 'Basket of Flowers Teacosy', page 12 in *The Australian Women's Mirror*, 7 December 1943, nla.obj-530623153.

Acknowledgements

Trove, the National Library of Australia's content aggregator, is an incredible source for vintage crochet patterns. All of the patterns in this book were found on Trove. The Library would like to thank *The Australian Women's Weekly* and Are Media for their contribution. The models are Library staff members and the children and friends of Library staff members. All photography for the book was done by the Library's photographers, Lindi Heap and Claire Williams. The Library would like to thank the following volunteers who crocheted and modelled for this book:

Crocheters

Alexis Mendoza
Anne Lewis
Beverly Burne
Cathy Aggett
Carol Clark
Catriona Bryce
Dania Warmerdam
Deborah Agapiou
Fiona Feeney
Fiona Moffatt
Harrison Swift
Inger Sundstorm
Karen Bailey
Karen Wray
Kataleeya Clarke
Katalin Mindum
Lesley Wilcox
Maretta Osgood
Melody Lord
Meredith D'Alton
Natasha Baker
Nicole Schwirtlich
Ngarie Curran
Suzanne de Smet

Models

Amelia Hartney
Bella Shaw
Cheney Brew
Cris Kennedy
Ella Morrison
Grace Baines
Hamish Hartney-Jones
Ivan Goranov
Judith Roga
Ky Kim
Maria Genetzakis
Mishka Sharma
Nicole Schwirtlich
Noel Brown
Samuel Hartney-Jones
Shelly McGuire
Shirley Hedditch

Published by National Library of Australia Publishing

Canberra ACT 2600

ISBN: 9781922507655

The National Library of Australia acknowledges Australia's First Nations Peoples—the First Australians—as the Traditional Owners and Custodians of this land and gives respect to the Elders—past and present—and through them to all Australian Aboriginal and Torres Strait Islander people.

Publisher: Lauren Smith
Managing editor: Amelia Hartney
Editor: Melody Lord
Designer: Astred Hicks, Design Cherry, with Hannah Janzen
Image coordinator: Madeleine Warburton
Printed in China by RR Donnelley on FSC®-certified paper.

Find out more about NLA Publishing at nla.gov.au/national-library-publishing.

A catalogue record for this book is available from the National Library of Australia